£32.14

PURE

Java Server Pages

.35

James Goodwill

SAMS

Pure Java Server Pages

Copyright © 2000 by Sams Publishing

International Standard Book Number: 0-672-31902-0

Library of Congress Catalog Card Number: 99-68590

Printed in the United States of America

First Printing: May 2000

02   01   00   4   3   2   1

Trademarks

Warning and Disclaimer

PUBLISHER
Michael Stephens

ACQUISITIONS EDITOR
Steve Anglin

DEVELOPMENT EDITOR
Tiffany Taylor

MANAGING EDITOR
Matt Purcell

PROJECT EDITOR
Paul Schneider

COPY EDITOR
Mary Ellen Stephenson

INDEXER
Rebecca Salerno

PROOFREADERS
Kaylene Riemen
Linda Morris

TECHNICAL EDITOR
Al Saganich

TEAM COORDINATOR
Pamalee Nelson

SOFTWARE SPECIALIST
Jason Haines

INTERIOR DESIGNER
Karen Ruggies

COVER DESIGNER
Aren Howell

COPYWRITER
Eric Borgert

LAYOUT TECHNICIANS
Stacey DeRome
Ayanna Lacey
Heather Hiatt Miller
Tim Osborn

Contents at a Glance

Contents

21 THE JAVAX.SERVLET.HTTP PACKAGE 269

Dedication

To Christy, Abby, and our unborn child.

Acknowledgments

I would first like to thank everyone at my company, Virtuas Solutions, Inc., for their support while I was completing this text. The entire staff contributed by picking up my assignments when my plate was too full. In particular I would like to thank those whom I worked with on a daily basis including Matthew Filios, Karen Jackson, Kothai Sengodan, Eric Johnson, and especially Aaron Bandell, for his contribution of the ShoppingCart bean in Chapter 13 and his introduction to the JavaMail API in Chapter 17.

I would also like to thank the people who helped me create this text. I would like to thank my Development Editor, Tiffany Taylor, who always had great input and suggestions as the book progressed. I would like to thank my Copy Editor, Mary Ellen Stephenson, for her insightful comments. I would also like to thank my Technical Editor, Al Saganich, for his technical suggestions. And last but not least, I would like to thank my Acquisitions Editor, Steve Anglin, for his continued efforts in getting things taken care of for me along the way.

Finally, the most important contributions to this book came from my wife, Christy, and our daughter, Abby. They supported me again throughout this text, my second book, with complete understanding. They provided time for me to write and support when I felt like I could not write anymore. They are truly the most important people in my life.

About the Author

James Goodwill is the Chief Internet Architect and a Principal at Virtuas Solutions, Inc., located in Denver, Colorado. He has extensive experience in telecommunications and e-business applications. James is also the author of *Developing Java Servlets*, a Sams Professional title, which provides a thorough look at Java servlets. Over the last several years he has been focusing his efforts on the design and development of electronic commerce applications.

Tell Us What You Think!

As the reader of this book, *you* are our most important critic and commentator. We value your opinion and want to know what we're doing right, what we could do better, what areas you'd like to see us publish in, and any other words of wisdom you're willing to pass our way.

As a Publisher for Sams, I welcome your comments. You can fax, email, or write me directly to let me know what you did or didn't like about this book—as well as what we can do to make our books stronger.

Please note that I cannot help you with technical problems related to the topic of this book, and that due to the high volume of mail I receive, I might not be able to reply to every message.

When you write, please be sure to include this book's title and author as well as your name and phone or fax number. I will carefully review your comments and share them with the author and editors who worked on the book.

Fax: 317-581-4770
Email: java@mcp.com
Mail: Michael Stephens
            Associate Publisher
            Sams Publishing
            201 West 103rd Street
            Indianapolis, IN 46290 USA

Introduction

How This Book Is Organized

Before you begin reading *Pure JSP Java Server Pages*, you might want to take a look at its basic structure. This should help you outline your reading plan if you choose not to read the text from cover to cover. This introduction gives you an overview of what each chapter covers.

Chapter 1, "JSP Overview: The Components of a JavaServer Page"

Chapter 1 takes a look at the basics of JSP and the components of JSPs. It shows you how to create a JSP document and helps you to understand what is happening behind the scenes at request-time. It also discusses the process a JSP file goes through when it is first requested.

Chapter 2, "Java Servlets"

Chapter 2 covers how to create, build, and install your own servlets. It also provides a basic understanding of the servlet life cycle and where your servlets will fit into the Java servlet framework.

Chapter 3, "JavaBeans and JSP Concepts"

Chapter 3 covers the basics of JavaBeans. It takes a look at the standard actions involved in embedding a bean within a JSP. It also covers the different types of scope in which a bean can exist.

Chapter 4, "JDBC and JSP Concepts"

Chapter 4 discusses the basics of the JDBC (Java Database Connectivity) interface and how to set up a JDBC driver. It also examines how you can incorporate the JDBC into a JSP and how you can break up your scriptlet code by embedding your HTML code into it.

Chapter 5, "Configuring the JSP Server"

Chapter 5 covers the necessary steps involved in installing and configuring the Tomcat server, including how you add a new Web Application.

Chapter 6, "Handling JSP Errors"

Chapter 6 covers the types of errors that can occur in a JSP. It also shows you how you can handle and respond to these errors, using a JSP error page.

Chapter 7, "Using the include Directive"

Chapter 7 covers how the JSP `include` directive works. It also discusses when the `include` directive is processed. After reading this chapter, you should know how to include a JSP or HTML file using the `include` directive; you should also know when included file changes take effect.

Chapter 8, "JavaServer Pages and Inheritance"

Chapter 8 discusses how you can subclass JSPs to provide common utility methods. It also covers the requirements of both the superclass and the JSP subclass.

Chapter 9, "Using the JSP's Implicit Objects"

Chapter 9 discusses the JSP implicit objects and how they are commonly used. It also talks about how they are created in the JSP's generated servlet.

Chapter 10, "Using JSP Standard Actions"

Chapter 10 covers the JSP standard actions, including how they are implemented and how you can use them.

Chapter 11, "JSPs and JavaBean Scope"

Chapter 11 covers how JSP beans are scoped. It discusses the different types of JSP scope. It also covers how the life of a JSP bean is determined by its scope.

Chapter 12, "JSP and HTML Forms"

Chapter 12 covers how you can retrieve form data using JSPs. It also discusses retrieving data from forms using either GET or POST requests.

Chapter 13, "JSP and a Shopping Cart"

Chapter 13 covers how to create, integrate, and use a shopping cart in a JSP.

Chapter 14, "JSP and a JDBC Connection Pool Bean"

Chapter 14 covers how to use a JDBC Connection Pool in a JSP. It also discusses how to share the pool with other JSPs by creating it with a scope of `application`.

Chapter 15, "JSP and XML"

Chapter 15 covers the basics of Extensible Markup Language, or XML. It discusses how to use Sun's SAX parser. It also shows an example of how you would incorporate XML and JSPs.

Chapter 16, "JSP Communication with Servlets"

Chapter 16 discusses the Model-View-Controller (MVC) design pattern. It talks about the drawbacks of a servlet or JSP-only application model. And finally it looks at how we can solve the problems encountered by the JSP- and servlet-only application models, by leveraging the MVC design pattern.

Chapter 17, "JSP and JavaMail"

Chapter 17 discusses what JavaMail is and how you use it with JSPs and other applications.

Chapter 18, "The javax.servlet.jsp Package"

Chapter 18 covers the classes, interfaces, and exceptions of the `javax.servlet.jsp` package.

Chapter 19, "The javax.servlet.jsp.tagext Package"

Chapter 19 covers the classes, interfaces, and exceptions of the `javax.servlet.jsp.tagext` package.

Chapter 20, "The javax.servlet Package"

Chapter 20 covers the classes, interfaces, and exceptions of the `javax.servlet` package.

Chapter 21, "The javax.servlet.http Package"

Chapter 21 covers the classes, interfaces, and exceptions of the `javax.servlet.http` package.

Source Code

You should also note that in several places you will see servlet code that was generated from a Java Server Page (JSP). This code is only given to show you how JSPs really work. It is meant to show how JSPs are truly just dynamically created servlets. The code generated is completely dependent on the JSP engine that is being used.

You can find the source code and support for this text at the Virtuas Solutions Web site, `http://www.virtuas.com/books.html`. You can also download the source code files from `www.samspublishing.com`. When you reach that page, click the Product Support link. On the next page, enter this book's ISBN number (0672319020) to access the page containing the code.

PART I

CONCEPTUAL REFERENCE

CHAPTER 1

JSP Overview: The Components of a JavaServer Page

JavaServer Pages, also known as JSPs, are a simple but powerful technology used to generate dynamic HTML on the server side. They are a direct extension of Java servlets and provide a way to separate content generation from content presentation. The JSP engine is just another servlet that is mapped to the extension *.jsp. The following code contains a simple example of a JSP file:

```
<HTML>
<BODY>

<% out.println("HELLO JSP WORLD"); %>

</BODY>
</HTML>
```

Its output would look similar to Figure 1.1.

You can see that this document looks like any other HTML document with some added tags containing Java code. The source code is stored in a file called HelloJSPWorld.jsp and copied to the document directory of the Web server. When a request is made for this document, the server recognizes the *.jsp extension and realizes that special handling is required. The first time the file is requested, it is compiled into a servlet object and stored in memory, and the output is sent back to the requesting client. After the first request, the server checks to see whether the *.jsp file has changed. If it has not changed, then the server invokes the previously compiled servlet object.

In this chapter and throughout the rest of the book, we will be discussing just how JSPs work and how to use them. Figure 1.2 shows these steps graphically.

Figure 1.1

Output of the JSP example.

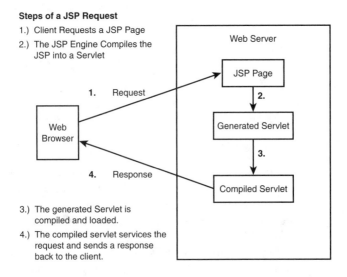

Steps of a JSP Request

1.) Client Requests a JSP Page

2.) The JSP Engine Compiles the JSP into a Servlet

3.) The generated Servlet is compiled and loaded.

4.) The compiled servlet services the request and sends a response back to the client.

Figure 1.2

The steps of a JSP request.

NOTE

A key thing to remember about JSPs is that they are just servlets that are created from a combination of HTML text and Java source code. This means that they contain all the functionality of a normal servlet.

The Components of a JavaServer Page

In this section we are going to cover the components that make up a JavaServer Page. They are discussed in detail in the following sections.

Directives

Directives are JSP elements that provide global information about an entire JSP page. An example would be a directive that indicated the language to be used in compiling a JSP page. The syntax of a directive is as follows:

```
<%@ directive {attribute="value"} %>
```

This states that, for *this* page directive, assign *these* values for *these* attributes. A directive can contain *n* number of optional attribute/value pairs.

If we use our previous example for indicating the JSP language, the following line of code would indicate that the JSP language to use would be Java:

```
<%@ page language="java" %>
```

There are three possible directives currently defined by the JSP specification: page, include, and taglib. Each one of these directives and their attributes, if applicable, are defined in the following sections.

The page Directive

The page directive defines information that will be globally available for that JavaServer Page. These page level settings will directly affect the compilation of the JSP. Table 1.1 defines the attributes for the page directive.

NOTE

Because the mandatory attributes are defaulted, you are not required to specify any page directives.

Table 1.1   The Attributes for the page Directive

Attribute	Definition
language="scriptingLanguage"	This attribute tells the server what language will be used to compile the JSP file. Currently Java is the only available language.

continues

Table 1.1   continued

Attribute	Definition
`extends="className"`	This attribute defines the parent class that the JSP generated servlet will extend from.
`import="importList"`	This attribute defines the list of packages that will be available to this JSP. It will be a comma-separated list of package names.
`session="true|false"`	This attribute determines whether the session data will be available to this page. The default is `true`.
`buffer="none|size in kb"`	This attribute determines whether the output stream is buffered. The default value is 8KB.
`autoFlush="true|false"`	This attribute determines whether the output buffer will be flushed automatically, or whether it will raise an exception when the buffer is full. The default is `true`, which states that the buffer should be flushed automatically.
`isThreadSafe="true|false"`	This attribute tells the JSP engine that this page can service more than one request at a time. By default this value is `true`; if `false`, the `SingleThreadModel` is used.
`info="text"`	This attribute represents information about the JSP page that can be accessed by the page's `Servlet.getServlet Info()` method.
`errorPage="error_url"`	This attribute represents the relative URL to the JSP page that will handle exceptions.
`isErrorPage="true|false"`	This attribute states whether or not the JSP page is an `errorPage`. The default is `false`.
`contentType="ctinfo"`	This attribute represents the MIME type and character set of the response.

The include Directive

The `include` directive is used to insert text and code at JSP translation time. The syntax of the `include` directive is as follows:

```
<%@ include file="relativeURLspec" %>
```

The file that the `file` attribute points to can reference a normal text HTML file or it can reference a JSP file, which will be evaluated at translation time.

NOTE

Currently the JSP 1.1 specification does not have a defined method for notifying the JSP engine that the included JSP file has changed.

The taglib Directive

The most recent version of the JSP specification defines a mechanism for extending the current set of JSP tags. It does this by creating a custom set of tags called a *tag library*. That is what the `taglib` points to. The `taglib` directive declares that the page uses custom tags, uniquely names the tag library defining them, and associates a tag prefix that will distinguish usage of those tags. The syntax of the `taglib` directive is as follows:

```
<%@ taglib uri="tagLibraryURI" prefix="tagPrefix" %>
```

The `taglib` attributes are described in Table 1.2.

Table 1.2 *The Attributes for the* `taglib` *Directive*

Attribute	Definition
uri	This attribute references a URI that uniquely names the set of custom tags.
prefix	This attribute defines the prefix string used to distinguish a custom tag instance.

Actions

Actions provide an abstraction that can be used to easily encapsulate common tasks. They typically create or act on objects, normally JavaBeans. The JSP technology provides some standard actions. These actions are defined in the following sections.

<jsp:useBean>

The `<jsp:useBean>` action associates an instance of a JavaBean defined with a given scope and ID, via a newly declared scripting variable of the same ID. The `<jsp:useBean>` action will be covered in more detail in Chapter 3, "JavaBeans and JSP Concepts."

<jsp:setProperty>

The `<jsp:setProperty>` action sets the value of a bean's property. The `<jsp:setProperty>` action will be covered in more detail in Chapter 3.

<jsp:getProperty>

The `<jsp:getProperty>` action takes the value of the referenced bean instance's property, converts it to a java.lang.String, and places it into the implicit out object. This action will be covered in more detail in Chapter 3.

<jsp:include>

The `<jsp:include>` action provides a mechanism for including additional static and dynamic resources in the current JSP page. The syntax for this action is as follows:

```
<jsp:include page="urlSpec" flush="true" />
```

and

```
<jsp:include page="urlSpec" flush="true">
    { jsp:param ... /> }
</jsp:include>
```

The first syntax example illustrates a request-time inclusion, whereas the second contains a list of param sub-elements that are used to argue the request for the purpose of inclusion. Table 1.3 contains the attributes and their descriptions for the <jsp:include> action.

Table 1.3   The Attributes for the <jsp:include> Action

Attribute	Definition
page	This attribute represents the relative URL of the resource to be included.
flush	This attribute represents a mandatory Boolean value, stating whether or not the buffer should be flushed.

<jsp:forward>

The <jsp:forward> action enables the JSP engine to dispatch, at runtime, the current request to a static resource, servlet, or another JSP. The appearance of this action effectively terminates the execution of the current page.

NOTE

A <jsp:forward> action can contain <jsp:param> sub-attributes. These sub-attributes provide values for parameters in the request to be used for forwarding.

The syntax of the <jsp:forward> action is as follows:

```
<jsp:forward page="relativeURLspec" />
```

and

```
<jsp:forward page=relativeURLspec">
    { <jsp:param .../> }
</jsp:forward>
```

Table 1.4 contains the single attribute and its descriptions for the <jsp:forward> action.

Table 1.4   The Attribute for the <jsp:forward> Action

Attribute	Definition
page	This attribute represents the relative URL of the target to be forwarded.

<jsp:param>

The `<jsp:param>` action is used to provide tag/value pairs of information, by including them as sub-attributes of the `<jsp:include>`, `<jsp:forward>`, and the `<jsp:plugin>` actions. The syntax of the `<jsp:param>` action is as follows:

```
<jsp:params>
    <jsp:param name="paramName"
    value="paramValue">
</jsp:params>
```

Table 1.5 contains the attributes and their descriptions for the `<jsp:param>` action.

Table 1.5   The Attributes for the `<jsp:param>` Action

Attribute	Definition
name	This attribute represents the name of the parameter being referenced.
value	This attribute represents the value of the named parameter.

<jsp:plugin>

The `<jsp:plugin>` action gives a JSP author the ability to generate HTML that contains the appropriate client-browser–dependent constructs, for example, OBJECT or EMBED, that will result in the download of a Java plug-in and subsequent execution of the specified applet or JavaBeans component.

The `<jsp:plugin>` tag is replaced by either an `<object>` or `<embed>` tag, as appropriate for the requesting user agent, and the new tag is written to the output stream of the response object. The attributes of the `<jsp:plugin>` action provide configuration data for the presentation of the element. The syntax of the `<jsp:plugin>` action is as follows:

```
<jsp:plugin type="pluginType"
    code="classFile"
    codebase="relativeURLpath">

    <jsp:params>
    ...
    </jsp:params>

</jsp:plugin>
```

Table 1.6 contains the attributes and their descriptions for the `<jsp:plugin>` action.

Table 1.6   The Attributes for the `<jsp:plugin>` Action

Attribute	Definition
type	This attribute represents the type of plug-in to include. An example of this would be an applet.
code	This attribute represents the name of the class that will be executed by the plug-in.
codebase	This attribute references the base or relative path of where the code attribute can be found.

The `<jsp:params>` attributes indicate the optional parameters that can be passed to the applet or JavaBeans component.

Implicit Objects

As a JSP author, you have access to certain implicit objects that are available for use in JSP documents, without being declared first. To satisfy the JSP specification, all JSP scripting languages must provide access to the objects defined in Table 1.7. Each of these implicit objects has a class or interface type defined in a core Java Development Kit (JDK) or Java Servlet Development Kit (JSDK).

Table 1.7   The JSP Implicit Objects

Implicit Variable	Type	Description	Scope
application	javax.servlet.Servlet Context	Represents the servlet context returned from a call to getServletConfig(). getContext()	Application
config	javax.servlet.Servlet Config	Represents the Servlet Config for this JSP	Page
exception	java.lang.Throwable	Represents the uncaught Throwable that resulted from a call to the error page	Page
out	javax.servlet.jsp. JspWriter	Represents the JspWriter object to the output stream	Page

Implicit Variable	Type	Description	Scope
page	java.lang.Object	Represents the this object for this instance of the JSP	Page
pageContext	javax.servlet.jsp. PageContext	Represents the page context for the JSP	Page
request	Protocol-dependent subtype of either javax.servlet.Servlet Request or javax. servlet.HttpServlet Request	Represents the request object that triggered the request	Request
response	Protocol-dependent subtype of either javax.servlet. ServletResponse or javax.servlet. HttpServletResponse	Represents the response object that triggered the request	Page
session	javax.servlet. http.HttpSession	Represents the session object, if any, created for the client during an HTTP request	Session

JSP Scripting

JSP scripting is a mechanism for embedding code fragments directly into an HTML page. There are three scripting language elements involved in JSP scripting. Each of these JSP scripting elements has its appropriate location in the generated servlet. In this section we will look at these elements and how together they will result in a complete servlet.

Declarations

JSP declarations are used to declare variables and methods in the scripting language used in a JSP page. A JSP declaration should be a complete declarative statement.

JSP declarations are initialized when the JSP page is initialized. After the declarations have been initialized, they are available to other declarations, expressions, and scriptlets. The syntax for a JSP declaration is as follows:

```
<%! declaration %>
```

A sample variable declaration using this syntax is declared here:

```
<%! String name = new String("BOB"); %>
```

A sample method declaration using the same syntax is declared as follows:

```
<%! public String getName() { return name; } %>
```

To get a better understanding of declarations, let's take the previous String declaration and actually use it to create a JSP document. The sample document would look similar to the following code snippet:

```
<HTML>
<BODY>

<%! String name = new String("BOB"); %>

</BODY>
</HTML>
```

When this document is initially requested, the JSP code is converted to servlet code and the previous declaration is placed in the declaration section of the generated servlet. The declarations section of the generated servlet would look similar to the following code snippet:

```
// begin [file="D:\\Declarations.jsp";from=(3,3);to=(3,37)]
String name = new String("BOB");
// end
```

Expressions

JSP expressions are elements in a scripting language that are evaluated with the result being converted to a java.lang.String. After the string is converted, it is written to the current out JspWriter object.

JSP expressions are evaluated at HTTP request-time, with the resulting String being inserted at the expression's referenced position in the .jsp file. If the resulting expression cannot be converted to a String, then a translation time error will occur. If the conversion to a String cannot be detected during translation, a ClassCastException will be thrown at request-time. The syntax of a JSP expression is as follows:

```
<%= expression %>
```

A code snippet containing a JSP expression is shown here:

```
Hello <B><%= getName() %></B>
```

To get a better understanding of expressions, let's take this snippet and insert it into a simple JSP document. The sample document would look similar to the following code snippet:

```
<HTML>
<BODY>

<%! String name = new String("BOB"); %>
<%! public String getName() { return name; } %>

Hello <B><%= getName() %></B>

</BODY>
</HTML>
```

When this document is initially requested, the JSP code is converted to servlet code and the previous expression is resolved and placed in its referenced location of the generated servlet's _jspService() method. The generated servlet would look similar to the following code snippet:

```
// begin
out.write("<HTML>\r\n<BODY>\r\n\r\n");
// end
// begin
out.write("\r\n");
// end
// begin
out.write("\r\n\r\nHello <B>");
// end
// begin [file="D:\\Expressions.jsp";from=(6,12);to=(6,23)]
out.print( getName() );
// end
// begin
out.write("</B>\r\n\r\n</BODY>\r\n</HTML>\r\n");
// end
```

Scriptlets

Scriptlets are what bring all the scripting elements together. They can contain any coding statements that are valid for the language referenced in the language directive. They are executed at request-time and they can make use of declarations, expressions, and JavaBeans. The syntax for a scriptlet is as follows:

```
<% scriptlet source %>
```

During the initial request the JSP scripting code is converted to servlet code and then compiled and loaded into resident memory. The actual source code, which is found between scriptlet tags <% ... %>, is placed into the newly created servlet's _jspService() method. See the following sample JSP source:

```
<HTML>
<BODY>

<% out.println("HELLO JSP WORLD"); %>
```

```
</BODY>
</HTML>
```

It has a very simple scriptlet section that will print *HELLO JSP WORLD* to the JspWriter implicit object out. The actual servlet code, resulting from the initial request, would look similar to the following code snippet:

```
public void _jspService(HttpServletRequest request,
HttpServletResponse  response)
  throws IOException, ServletException {

  JspFactory _jspxFactory = null;
  PageContext pageContext = null;
  HttpSession session = null;
  ServletContext application = null;
  ServletConfig config = null;
  JspWriter out = null;
  Object page = this;
  String  _value = null;

  try {

    if (_jspx_inited == false) {
        _jspx_init();
        _jspx_inited = true;
    }
    _jspxFactory = JspFactory.getDefaultFactory();
    response.setContentType("text/html");
    pageContext = _jspxFactory.getPageContext(this,
      request, response,
      "", true, 8192, true);

    application = pageContext.getServletContext();
    config = pageContext.getServletConfig();
    session = pageContext.getSession();
    out = pageContext.getOut();

    // begin
    out.write("<HTML>\r\n<BODY>\r\n\r\n");
    // end
    // begin [file="D:\\HelloJsp.jsp";from=(3,2);to=(3,35)]
    out.println("HELLO JSP WORLD");
    // end
    // begin
    out.write("\r\n\r\n</BODY>\r\n</HTML>\r\n");
    // end
    }
    catch (Exception ex) {
```

```
      if (out.getBufferSize() != 0)
        out.clear();
      pageContext.handlePageException(ex);
   }
   finally {

      out.flush();
      jspxFactory.releasePageContext(pageContext);
   }
}
```

You don't need to dig too deeply into this code, because it is generated for you. You just need to understand that it is being generated by the JSP engine and is the JSP equivalent to a servlet's `service()` method. It is also important to know that the JSP engine creates a servlet equivalent to the `init()` and `destroy()` methods. We will take a look at these methods in the later technique chapters.

Summary

In this chapter we covered quite a bit of information. We took a look at the different types of JSP application models. We also covered the basics of JSPs and the components of JSPs. You now should be able to create a JSP document and understand what is happening behind the scenes during request-time. You should also understand the process a JSPsfile goes through when it is first requested.

In Chapter 2, "Java Servlets," we are going to cover Java servlets. Then in Chapter 3, "JavaBeans and JSP Concepts," we'll look at JavaBeans and how they can be used in JSPs.

CHAPTER 2

Java Servlets

JavaServer Pages are extensions of Java servlets, therefore, you really need to understand Java servlets before you can fully grasp the JSP architecture. Given the previous statement, servlets are generic extensions to Java-enabled servers. Their most common use is to extend Web servers, providing a very efficient, portable, and easy-to-use replacement for CGI. A *servlet* is a dynamically loaded module that services requests from a Web server. It runs entirely inside the Java Virtual Machine. Because the servlet is running on the server side, it does not depend on browser compatibility. Figure 2.1 depicts the execution of a Java servlet. In this chapter, you'll learn the basics of working with servlets, and how servlets fit into the framework of JSP.

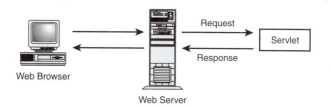

Figure 2.1

Execution of a Java servlet.

Practical Applications for Java Servlets

Servlets can be used for any number of "Web-related" applications. When you start using servlets, you will find more practical applications for them. The following list contains three examples that I believe are some of the most important applications:

- Developing e-commerce "storefronts" will become one of the most common uses for Java servlets. A servlet can build an online catalog based on the contents of a database. It can then present this catalog to the customer using dynamic HTML. The customer will choose the items to be ordered, enter the shipping and billing information, and then submit the data to a servlet. When the servlet receives the posted data, it will process the orders and place them in the database for fulfillment. Every one of these processes can easily be implemented using Java servlets.
- Servlets can be used to deploy Web sites that open up large legacy systems on the Internet. Many companies have massive amounts of data stored on large mainframe systems, These businesses do not want to reengineer their systems' architecture, so they choose to provide inexpensive Web interfaces into the systems. Because you have the entire JDK at your disposal and security provided by the Web server, you can use servlets to interface into these systems using anything from TCP/IP to CORBA.
- When developing a distributed object application that will be deployed to the Web, you run into access issues. If you choose to use applets in your client browser, you are only able to open a connection to the originating server, which might be behind a firewall. Getting through a firewall using Remote Method Invocation (RMI) is a very common problem. If servlets are employed, you can tunnel through the firewall using a servlet technology called HTTPTunneling. This enables the applet to access objects that can be running almost anywhere on the network.

These are just a few examples of the power and practicality of using Java servlets. Servlets are a very viable option for most Web applications.

The Java Servlet Architecture

Two packages make up the servlet architecture: the `javax.servlet` and `javax.servlet.http` packages. The `javax.servlet` package contains the generic interfaces and classes that are implemented and extended by all servlets. The `javax.servlet.http` package contains the classes that are extended when creating HTTP-specific servlets. An example of this would be a simple servlet that responds using HTML.

At the heart of this architecture is the interface `javax.servlet.Servlet`. It provides the framework for all servlets. The `Servlet` interface defines five methods. The three most important are as follows:

- `init()` method—Initializes a servlet
- `service()` method—Receives and responds to client requests
- `destroy()` method—Performs cleanup

All servlets must implement this interface, either directly or through inheritance. It is a very clean object-oriented approach that makes the interface very easy to extend. Figure 2.2 is an object model that gives you a very high-level view of the servlet framework.

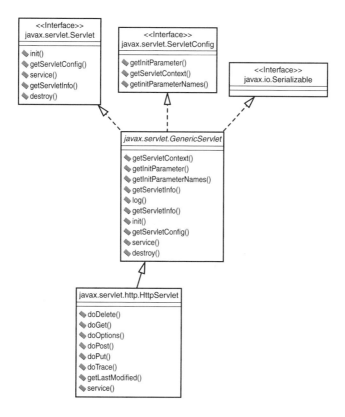

Figure 2.2

A high-level object model of the servlet framework.

GenericServlet and HttpServlet

The two main classes are the GenericServlet and HttpServlet classes. The HttpServlet class is extended from GenericServlet. When you are developing your own servlets, you will most likely be extending one of these two classes. If you are going to be creating Web Applications, then you will be extending the HttpServlet class. Java servlets do not have a main() method, which is why all servlets must implement the javax.servlet.Servlet interface. Every time a server receives a request that points to a servlet, it calls that servlet's service() method.

If you decide to extend the GenericServlet class, you must implement the service() method. The GenericServlet.service() method has been defined as an abstract method in order to force you to follow this framework. The service() method prototype is defined as follows:

```
public abstract void service(ServletRequest req,
ServletResponse res) throws ServletException, IOException;
```

The two objects that the service() method receives are ServletRequest and ServletResponse. The ServletRequest object holds the information that is being sent to the servlet, whereas the ServletResponse object is where you place the data you want to send back to the server. Figure 2.3 diagrams the flow of a GenericServlet request.

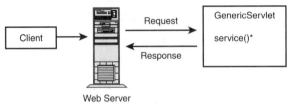

Figure 2.3

A GenericServlet *request.*

Unlike with GenericServlet, when you extend HttpServlet, you don't usually implement the service() method. The HttpServlet class has already implemented it for you. The following is the prototype:

```
protected void service(HttpServletRequest req, HttpServletResponse resp)
throws ServletException, IOException;
```

When the HttpServlet.service() method is invoked, it reads the method type stored in the request and determines which method to invoke based upon this value. These are the methods that you will want to override. If the method type is GET, it will call doGet(). If the method type is POST, it will call doPost(). There are five other method types and these will be covered later in this chapter. All these methods have the same parameter list as the service() method.

You might have noticed the different request/response types in the parameter list of the HttpServlet versus the GenericServlet class. The HttpServletRequest and HttpServletResponse classes are just extensions of ServletRequest and ServletResponse with HTTP-specific information stored in them. Figure 2.4 diagrams the flow of an HttpServlet request.

The Life Cycle of a Servlet

The life cycle of a Java servlet is a very simple object-oriented design. A servlet is constructed and initialized. It then services zero or more requests until the service that it extends shuts down. At this point the servlet is destroyed and garbage collected. This design explains why servlets are such a good replacement for CGI. The servlet is loaded only once and it stays resident in memory while servicing requests.

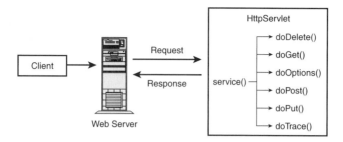

Figure 2.4

An HttpServlet *request*

The interface that declares this framework is the javax.servlet.Servlet interface. The Servlet interface defines the life cycle methods. These methods are init(), service(), and destroy().

init()

The init() method is where the servlet's life begins. It is called by the server immediately after the servlet is instantiated. It is called only once. In the init() method, the servlet creates and initializes any resources, including data members, that it will be using while handling requests. The init() method's signature is defined as follows:

```
public void init(ServletConfig config) throws ServletException;
```

The init() method takes a ServletConfig object as a parameter. You should save this object so that it can be referenced later. The most common way of doing this is to have the init() method call super.init(), passing it the ServletConfig object.

You will also notice that the init() method can throw a ServletException. If, for some reason, the servlet cannot initialize the resources necessary to handle requests, the init() method will throw a ServletException.

service()

The service() method handles all requests sent by a client. It cannot start servicing requests until the init() method has been executed. You will not usually implement this method directly, unless you extend the GenericServlet abstract class.

The most common implementation of the service() method is in the HttpServlet class. The HttpServlet class implements the Servlet interface by extending GenericServlet. Its service() method supports standard HTTP/1.1 requests by determining the request type and calling the appropriate method. The signature of the service() method is as follows:

```
public void service(ServletRequest req, ServletResponse res)
throws ServletException, IOException;
```

The service() method implements a request and response paradigm. The ServletRequest object contains information about the service request, encapsulating information provided by the client. The ServletResponse object contains the information returned to the client.

destroy()

This method signifies the end of a servlet's life. When a service is being shut down, it calls the servlet's destroy() method. This is where any resources that were created in the init() method will be cleaned up. If you have an open database connection, you should close it here. This is also a good place to save any persistent information that will be used the next time the servlet is loaded. The signature of the destroy() is very simple, but I have displayed it here just to complete the picture:

```
public void destroy();
```

A Basic Servlet

In this section, we are going to look at building and running a very basic servlet. Its purpose will be to service a request and respond with the request method used by the client. We will take a quick look at the servlet's source code, the steps involved in compiling and installing the servlet, and the HTML necessary to invoke the servlet.

The BasicServlet Source

Listing 2.1 contains the source code for this example. You can find the following source listing on this book's Web site. If you have the time, it is probably best if you type the first few examples yourself. This will help you become familiar with the basic parts of servlets.

Listing 2.1   BasicServlet.java Displays the Request Method Used by the Client

```
import javax.servlet.*;
import javax.servlet.http.*;
import java.io.*;
import java.util.*;

public class BasicServlet extends HttpServlet {

  public void init(ServletConfig config)
    throws ServletException {

    // Always pass the ServletConfig object to the super class
    super.init(config);
  }

  //Process the HTTP Get request
  public void doGet(HttpServletRequest request,
    HttpServletResponse response)
    throws ServletException, IOException {
```

```
    response.setContentType("text/html");
    PrintWriter out = response.getWriter();

    out.println("<html>");
    out.println("<head><title>BasicServlet</title></head>");
    out.println("<body>");

    // Prints the REQUEST_METHOD sent by the client
    out.println("Your request method was " + request.getMethod()
      + "\n");

    out.println("</body></html>");
    out.close();
  }

  //Process the HTTP Post request
  public void doPost(HttpServletRequest request,
    HttpServletResponse response)
    throws ServletException, IOException {

    response.setContentType("text/html");
    PrintWriter out = response.getWriter();

    out.println("<html>");
    out.println("<head><title>BasicServlet</title></head>");
    out.println("<body>");

// Prints the REQUEST_METHOD sent by the client
    out.println("Your request method was " + request.getMethod()
      + "\n");

    out.println("</body></html>");
    out.close();
  }

//Get Servlet information
  public String getServletInfo() {

    return "BasicServlet Information";
  }
}
```

The HTML Required to Invoke the Servlet

This servlet implements both the doGet() and the doPost() methods. Therefore there are two ways to invoke this servlet.

The first is to just reference the servlet by name in the URL. The following URL will execute the servlet on my local server:

```
http://localhost/servlet/BasicServlet
```

Using this method defaults the request method to GET, which will invoke the servlet's doGet() method.

The second way to invoke the servlet is to create an HTML page that will send a request to the servlet using the POST method. This will invoke the servlet's doPost() method. Listing 2.2 shows the HTML listing to complete this task.

Listing 2.2   BasicServlet.html Displays the HTML Required to Invoke the Servlet Using the POST Method

```
<HTML>
<HEAD>
<TITLE>
BasicServlet
</TITLE>
</HEAD>
<BODY>

<FORM
  ACTION=http://localhost/servlet/BasicServlet
  METHOD=POST>

  <BR><BR>
  press Submit Query to launch servlet BasicServlet
  <BR><BR>
  <INPUT TYPE=submit>
  <INPUT TYPE=reset>
</FORM>

</BODY>
</HTML>
```

When you invoke the servlet using either of these methods, the results will be similar to Figure 2.5. The only notable difference will be the request method returned.

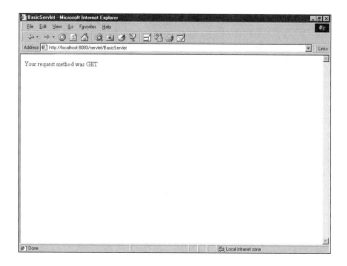

Figure 2.5

The BasicServlet *HTML response page.*

Dissecting the BasicServlet

Now that you have the BasicServlet installed and running, let's take a closer look at each of its integral parts. We will be examining the location where the servlet fits into the framework, methods the servlet implements, and the objects being used by the servlet.

Where Does the BasicServlet Fit into the Servlet Framework?

The first thing we are going to look at is where the BasicServlet fits into the servlet framework. This servlet extends the HttpServlet class. The HttpServlet class is an abstract class that simplifies writing HTTP servlets. It extends the GenericServlet class and provides the functionality for handling HTTP protocol-specific requests. The BasicServlet overrides four of its inherited methods. Figure 2.6 shows where the BasicServlet fits into this hierarchy.

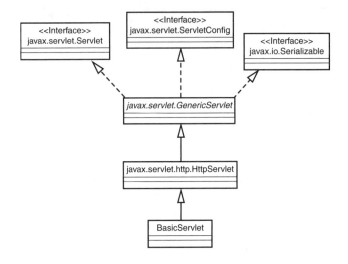

Figure 2.6

The BasicServlet *depicted in the framework.*

The Methods Overridden by the BasicServlet

The following four methods are overridden by the BasicServlet:

- init()
- doGet()
- doPost()
- getServletInfo()

Let's take a look at each of these methods in more detail.

init()

The BasicServlet defines a very simple implementation of the init() method. It takes the ServletConfig object that is passed to it and passes it to its parent's init() method, which stores the object for later use. The parent that actually holds onto the ServletConfig object is the GenericServlet class. GenericServlet provides your servlet, through inheritance, with methods to access the ServletConfig object. The code that performs this action follows:

```
super.init(config);
```

This is a very important step. If you do not do this, you must hold a reference to the ServletConfig object yourself.

You will also notice this implementation of the init() method does not create any resources. This is why the BasicServlet does not implement a destroy() method.

doGet() and doPost()

The BasicServlet's doGet() and doPost() methods are identical. The only difference is the requests they service. The doGet() method handles GET requests, and the doPost() method handles POST requests.

Both of these methods receive HttpServletRequest and HttpServletResponse objects. These objects encapsulate the request/response paradigm. The HttpServletRequest contains information sent from the client and the HttpServletResponse contains the information that will be sent back to the client. The first executed line of these methods is listed as follows:

```
response.setContentType("text/html");
```

This method sets the content type for the response. You can set this response property only once. You must set this property before you can begin writing to a Writer or an OutputStream. In our example, we are using a PrintWriter and setting the response type to text/html.

The next thing to do is get a reference to the PrintWriter. This is accomplished by calling the ServletRequest's getWriter() method. This is done in the following line of code:

```
PrintWriter out = response.getWriter();
```

Now you have a reference to an object that will enable you to write HTML text that will be sent back to the client in the HttpServletResponse object. The next few lines of code show how this is done:

```
out.println("<html>");
out.println("<head><title>BasicServlet</title></head>");
out.println("<body>");

// Prints the REMOTE_METHOD sent by the client in the request
out.println("Your request method was " + request.getMethod()
    + "\n");

out.println("</body></html>");
out.close();
```

This is a very straightforward method of sending HTML text back to the client. You simply pass to the PrintWriter's println() method the HTML text you want included in the response and close the stream. The only thing that you might have a question about is the following few lines:

```
// Prints the REMOTE_METHOD sent by the client in the request
out.println("Your request method was " + request.getMethod()
    + "\n");
```

This takes advantage of the information sent from the client. It calls the HttpServletRequest's getMethod() method, which returns the HTTP method with which the request, either GET/POST, was made. The HttpServletRequest object holds HTTP-protocol specific header information.

getServletInfo()

The final method overridden in the BasicServlet is getServletInfo(). This method is like the applet's getAppletInfo() method. It can be used to provide version, copyright, author, and any other information about itself.

Summary

You should now be able to create, build, and install your own servlets. You should also have a basic understanding of the servlet life cycle and where your servlets will fit into the Java Servlet framework. This is very important knowledge in understanding how JavaServer Pages work. You will be putting this information to use as we progress in the study of JSPs.

In Chapter 3, "JavaBeans and JSP Concepts," we begin to really take a look at the JavaServer Pages technology. Some of the topics we will cover include JSP application models, syntax, semantics, scripting, and directives.

CHAPTER 3

JavaBeans and JSP Concepts

Before we can start learning about how you can use JavaBeans in JavaServer Pages, we must take a look at what a bean is. A JavaBean is a 100% Java component that works on any Java Virtual Machine. The minimum requirements that make a component a JavaBean are as follows:

- It must support the JDK 1.1 and later Serialization model.
- It must use get/set accessors to expose its properties.

There is nothing magical about creating a JavaBean. You just create a Java class that implements the java.io. Serializable interface and uses public get/set methods to expose its properties. Listing 3.1 contains a simple JavaBean.

Listing 3.1 SimpleJavaBean.java

```
import java.io.Serializable;
public class SimpleJavaBean implements
java.io.Serializable{
  private String simpleProperty = new String("");
  public SimpleJavaBean() {

  }

  public String getSimpleProperty() {
    return simpleProperty;
  }

  public void setSimpleProperty(String value) {
    simpleProperty = value;
  }
}
```

This class is now a JavaBean. It satisfies the minimum requirements. You can now load the SimpleJavaBean into any JavaBeans–aware program that uses introspection and change its properties. Its state can then be saved and reloaded anytime, because of its support for serialization.

Let's take a look at an example that illustrates how to serialize our new bean. The example in Listing 3.2 creates an instance of our SimpleJavaBean, sets the simpleProperty to "simple property value", serializes the bean to a file, reads the bean back in, and finally displays proof that its state was maintained.

Listing 3.2 SimpleJavaBeanTester.java

```
import java.io.*;
public class SimpleJavaBeanTester {
  public SimpleJavaBeanTester() {

  }

  public void storeBean(SimpleJavaBean value) {
    try {
      // Create the ObjectOutputStream passing it the
      // FileOutputStream object that points to our
      // persistent storage.
      ObjectOutputStream os = new ObjectOutputStream(
        new FileOutputStream("file.dat"));
      // Write the SimpleJavaBean to the ObjectOutputStream
      os.writeObject(value);
      os.flush();
      os.close();
    }
    catch (IOException ioe) {
      System.err.println(ioe.getMessage());
    }
  }

  public SimpleJavaBean getBean() {
    SimpleJavaBean value = null;
    try {
      // Create the ObjectInputStream passing it the
      // FileInputStream object that points to our
      // persistent storage.
      ObjectInputStream is = new ObjectInputStream(
        new FileInputStream("file.dat"));
      // Read the stored object and downcast it back to
      // a SimpleJavaBean
      value = (SimpleJavaBean)is.readObject();
      is.close();
    }
    catch (IOException ioe) {
      System.err.println(ioe.getMessage());
```

```
    }
    catch (ClassNotFoundException cnfe) {
      System.err.println(cnfe.getMessage());
    }
    return value;
  }

  public void testBean() {
    // Create the Bean
    SimpleJavaBean simpleBean = new SimpleJavaBean();
    // Use accessor to set property
    simpleBean.setSimpleProperty("simple property value");
    // Serialize the Bean to a Persistent Store
    storeBean(simpleBean);
    // Get the Bean from the Persistent Store
    SimpleJavaBean newBean = getBean();
    System.out.println("The newBean's simpleProperty == " +
      newBean.getSimpleProperty());
  }

  public static void main(String[] args) {
    SimpleJavaBeanTester simpleJavaBeanTester =
      new SimpleJavaBeanTester();
    simpleJavaBeanTester.testBean();
    try {
      System.out.println("Press enter to continue...");
      System.in.read();
    }
    catch (IOException ioe) {
      System.err.println(ioe.getMessage());
    }
  }
}
```

If you build and run this application, the output will look similar to the following:

```
The newBean's simpleProperty == simple property value
Press enter to continue...
```

Adding JavaBeans to JavaServer Pages

Now that we understand what JavaBeans are and how they are commonly used, let's take a look at embedding them into JavaServer Pages. In the following sections, we are going to look at the standard actions used to reference JavaBeans and an example that uses these actions.

JavaBean Standard Actions

There are three standard actions defined to help integrate JavaBeans into JSPs: <jsp:useBean>, <jsp:setProperty>, and <jsp:getProperty>.

<jsp:useBean>

The first standard action is <jsp:useBean>. It associates an instance of a JavaBean defined with a given scope and id via a newly declared scripting variable of the same id.

The <jsp:useBean> action is very flexible. Its exact semantics depend on the values of the given attributes. The basic action tries to find an existing object using the same id and scope. If it does not find an existing instance, it will attempt to create the object. It is also possible to use this action only to give a local name to an object defined elsewhere, as in another JSP page or in a servlet. This can be done by using the type attribute, and by not providing the class or the beanName attribute. The syntax of the <jsp:useBean> action is as follows:

```
<jsp:useBean id="name"
        scope="page|request|session|application"
        typeSpec>
        body
</jsp:useBean>

typeSpec ::=class="className" |
        class="className" type="typeName" |
        type="typeName" class="className" |
        beanName="beanName" type="typeName" |
        type="typeName" beanName="beanName" |
        type="typeName"
```

Table 3.1 contains the attributes of the <jsp:useBean> action.

Table 3.1   The Attributes for the <jsp:useBean> *Action*

Attribute	Definition
id	This attribute represents the identity of the instance of the object in the specified scope. The name is case sensitive and must satisfy the current scripting language's variable naming conventions.
scope	The scope attribute represents the life of the object. The scope options are page, request, session, and application.
class	The fully qualified class name that defines the implementation of the object. The class name is case sensitive.
beanName	This attribute references the name of the bean, as expected to be instantiated by the instantiate() method of the java.beans.Beans class.
type	The type attribute specifies the type of scripting variable defined. If this attribute is unspecified, then the value is the same as the value of the class attribute.

<jsp:setProperty>

The second standard action to help integrate JavaBeans into JSPs is `<jsp:setProperty>`. It sets the value of a bean's property. Its `name` attribute denotes an object that must already be defined and in scope. The syntax for the `<jsp:setProperty>` action is as follows:

```
<jsp:setProperty name="beanName" prop_expr />
```

In the preceding syntax, the `name` attribute represents the name of the bean whose property you are setting, and *prop_expr* can be represented in the following syntax:

```
property="*" |
property="propertyName" |
property="propertyName" param="parameterName" |
property="propertyName" value="propertyValue"
```

Table 3.2 contains the attributes and their descriptions for the `<jsp:setProperty>` action.

Table 3.2   The Attributes for the `<jsp:setProperty>` *Action*

Attribute	Definition
name	This attribute represents the name of the bean instance defined by a `<jsp:useBean>` action or some other action.
property	This attribute represents the bean property for which you want to set a value. If you set *propertyName* to an asterisk (*), then the action will iterate over the current `ServletRequest` parameters, matching parameter names and value types to property names and setter method types, and setting each matched property to the value of the matching parameter. If a parameter has an empty string for a value, the corresponding property is left unmodified.
param	The `param` attribute represents the name of the request parameter whose value you want to set the named property to. A `<jsp:setProperty>` action cannot have both `param` and `value` attributes referenced in the same action.
value	The `value` attribute represents the value assigned to the named bean's property.

<jsp:getProperty>

The last standard action that references JavaBeans in JSPs is `<jsp:getProperty>`. It takes the value of the referenced bean instance's property, converts it to a `java.lang.String`, and places it into the implicit out object. The referenced bean instance must be defined and in scope before this action references it. The syntax for the `<jsp:getProperty>` action is as follows:

```
<jsp:getProperty name="name" property="propertyName" />
```

Table 3.3 contains the attributes and their descriptions for the <jsp:getProperty> action.

Table 3.3   The Attributes for the <jsp:getProperty> Action

Attribute	Definition
name	This attribute represents the name of the bean instance, from which the property is obtained, defined by a <jsp:useBean> action or some other action.
property	This attribute represents the bean property for which you want to get a value.

A JSP Example Using JavaBeans

In our example, we are going to use a simple JavaBean that acts as a counter. It has a single int property, count, that holds the current number of times the bean's property has been accessed. It also contains the appropriate methods for getting and setting this property. Listing 3.3 contains the source code for the Counter bean.

Listing 3.3   Counter.java

```java
public class Counter {

  // Initialize the bean on creation
  int count = 0;

  // Parameterless Constructor
  public Counter() {

  }

  // Property Getter
  public int getCount() {

    // Increment the count property, with every request
    count++;

    return this.count;
  }

  // Property Setter
  public void setCount(int count) {

    this.count = count;
  }
}
```

Now that we have defined our bean, let's look at how to integrate it into a JSP. Listing 3.4 contains the JSP that will use the Counter bean.

Listing 3.4 `BeanCounter.jsp`

```
<HTML>
<HEAD>
<TITLE>JSP Bean Example</TITLE>
</HEAD>

<BODY>

<!-- Set the scripting language to java -->
<%@ page language="java" %>
<%@ page import="Counter" %>

<!-- Instantiate the Counter bean with an id of "counter" -->
<jsp:useBean id="counter" scope="session" class="Counter" />

<!-- Set the bean's count property to the value of -->
<!-- the request parameter "count", using the -->
<!-- jsp:setProperty action. -->
<jsp:setProperty name="counter" property="count" param="count" />

<%

    // write the current value of the property count
    out.println("Count from scriptlet code : "
      + counter.getCount() + "<BR>");

%>

<!-- Get the bean's count property, -->
<!-- using the jsp:getProperty action. -->
Count from jsp:getProperty :
  <jsp:getProperty name="counter" property="count" /><BR>

</BODY>
</HTML>
```

In the `BeanCounter.jsp` page, we perform five actions that give examples of using beans in a JSP. We first tell the JSP engine that the scripting language we are using is Java, with the following snippet:

```
<%@ page language="java" %>
```

We then create an instance of the class `Counter`, with a `scope` of `session`, and assign it an `id` of `counter`. We do this using the standard action `<jsp:useBean>`. Now we can reference this bean, by using the name `counter`, throughout the rest of our JSP. The code snippet that creates the bean is as follows:

```
<jsp:useBean id="counter" scope="session" class="Counter" />
```

The third action we take is to set the bean's count property to the value of the count parameter, if it exists in the request. The code snippet that performs this action is as follows:

```
<!-- Set the bean's count property to the value of -->
<!-- the request parameter "count", using the -->
<!-- jsp:setProperty action. -->
<jsp:setProperty name="counter" property="count" param="count" />
```

In this snippet, we use the <jsp:setProperty> standard action to set the value of the count property. We do this by setting the name attribute to the name of the bean we want to reference, the property attribute to the name of the property to be set, and the param attribute to the name of the request parameter we want to set the property to.

The final two actions we perform show how you can get the current value of a bean's property. The first of these two examples uses a scriptlet. It simply accesses the bean by its referenced name counter and calls the getCount() method, just as any other Java code would. The scriptlet snippet is listed here:

```
<%

    // write the current value of the property count
    out.println("Count from scriptlet code : "
      + counter.getCount() + "<BR>");

%>
```

The second example uses the <jsp:getProperty> standard action, which requires the name of the bean and the property to be accessed. The action takes the attribute, calls the appropriate accessor, and embeds the results directly into the resulting HTML document, as shown in the following:

```
<!-- Get the bean's count property, -->
<!-- using the jsp:getProperty action. -->
Count from jsp:getProperty :
  <jsp:getProperty name="counter" property="count" /><BR>
```

Notice that the second reference to the count property results in a value that is one greater than the first reference. This is because both methods of accessing the count property result in a call to the getCount() method, which increments the value of count.

Another thing you might want to try is changing the value of the <jsp:useBean> action's scope attribute. This will affect the life of the bean and the value of the count property in the previous example. The available options are described in Table 3.4.

Table 3.4   *The* `scope` *Values for the* `<jsp:useBean>` *Action*

Value	Definition
page	Objects with `page` scope are accessible only within the page where they were created. References to an object with `page` scope will be released when the response is sent back to the client or the request is forwarded to another resource. Objects with `page` scope are stored in the `pagecontext`.
request	Objects with `request` scope are accessible only within pages processing the same request in which the object was created. References to the object will be released after the request is processed completely. If the request is forwarded to a resource in the same runtime, the object is still in scope. References to objects with `request` scope are stored in the `request` object.
session	Objects with `session` scope are accessible only within pages processing requests that are in the same session as the one in which the bean was created. It is illegal to define an object with `session` scope within a page if that page's `page` directive has the `session` attribute set equal to `false` (see Table 1.1 in Chapter 1). References to the `session` objects will be released after their associated sessions end. Objects with `session` scope are stored in the `session` object associated with the page activation.
application	Objects with `application` scope are accessible within pages processing requests that are in the same application space as the page in which they were created. References to the object will be released when the runtime environment reclaims the `ServletContext`. Objects with `application` scope can be defined and reached within pages that are not session-aware. References to objects with `application` scope are stored in the `application` object associated with the page.

Summary

In this chapter, we covered the basics of JavaBeans. We looked at the standard actions involved in embedding a bean within a JSP. We also covered the different types of scope in which a bean can exist.

You now should be able to create a JavaBean and access the bean within a JSP. You should also have a basic understanding of how the bean's scope affects its current state.

In Chapter 4, "JDBC and JSP Concepts," we are going to cover how you can perform JDBC operations within JSPs.

CHAPTER 4

JDBC and JSP Concepts

The JDBC (short for Java Database Connectivity) interface is a pure Java API used to execute SQL statements. This chapter will introduce the JDBC and then explore how to use it in JavaServer Pages.

The JDBC provides a set of classes and interfaces that can be used by developers to write database applications. Basic JDBC interaction, in its simplest form, can be broken down into four steps:

1. Open a connection to the database.
2. Execute a SQL statement.
3. Process the results.
4. Close the connection to the database.

The following code fragment shows these steps in action:

```
// Step 1. Open a connection to the ODBC datasource
titles.
con = DriverManager.getConnection("jdbc:odbc:titles",
    "admin", "password");

// Step 2. Execute the SQL statement.
Statement statement = con.createStatement();

ResultSet rs = statement.executeQuery("SELECT * " +
  "FROM Types");

// Step 3. Process the Results
while ( rs.next() ) {

    // get the type_id, which is an int
    System.err.println("Type ID = " +
rs.getInt("type_id"));
    // get the type_name, which is a String
```

```
    System.err.println("Type Name = " + rs.getString("type_name"));
}


// Step 4. Close the Connection.
rs.close();
con.close();
```

Two- and Three-Tier Database Access Models

The JDBC provides support for two- and three-tier database access models. We are going to examine both in this section.

When you use the two-tier database access model, your Java application talks directly to the database. This is accomplished through the use of a JDBC driver, which sends commands directly to the database. The results of these commands are then sent back from the database directly to the application. Figure 4.1 shows the two-tier model.

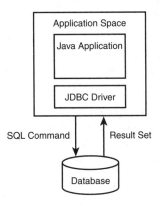

Figure 4.1

The two-tier JDBC model.

The three-tier model, as you might have guessed, is a little more complicated. When you use the three-tier model, your JDBC driver sends commands to a middle-tier, which in turn sends commands to the database. The results of these commands are then sent back to the middle-tier, which communicates them back to the application. Figure 4.2 shows the three-tier model.

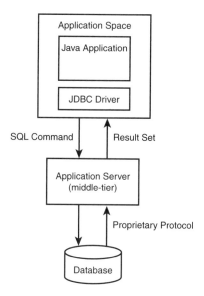

Figure 4.2

The three-tier JDBC model.

JDBC Driver Types

Sun has defined four JDBC driver types:

- JDBC-ODBC Bridge, plus ODBC driver
- Native-API, partly-Java driver
- JDBC-net, pure Java driver
- Native-protocol, pure Java driver

Each of these types meets a different application need, as we'll discuss in the following sections.

Type 1: JDBC-ODBC Bridge, Plus ODBC Driver

The first type of JDBC driver is the JDBC-ODBC Bridge. This driver type is provided by Sun with the JDK 1.1 and later. It provides JDBC access to databases through ODBC drivers. The ODBC driver must be configured on the client for the bridge to work. This driver type is commonly used for prototyping or when there is no JDBC driver available for a particular Database Management System (DBMS). Figure 4.3 shows the driver interaction of the JDBC-ODBC Bridge.

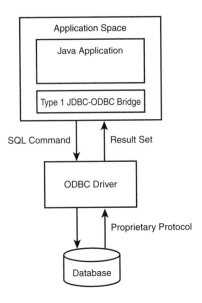

Figure 4.3

The Type 1 JDBC-ODBC Bridge.

Type 2: Native-API Driver

The native-API driver converts JDBC commands into DBMS-specific native calls. This is much like the restriction of Type 1 drivers. The client must have some binary code loaded on its machine. These drivers do have an advantage over Type 1 drivers, because they interface directly with the database. Figure 4.4 shows the interactions of a Type 2 driver.

Type 3: JDBC-Net, Pure Java Driver

The JDBC-Net drivers are a three-tier solution. This type of driver translates JDBC calls into a database-independent network protocol that is sent to a middleware server. This server then translates this DBMS-independent protocol into a DBMS-specific protocol, which is sent to a particular database. The results are routed back through the middleware server and sent back to the client. This type of solution makes it possible to implement a pure Java client. It also makes it possible to swap databases without affecting the client. This is by far the most flexible JDBC solution. Figure 4.4 shows this three-tier solution.

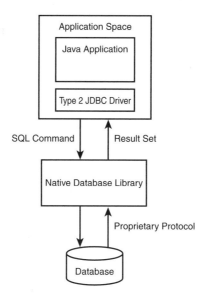

Figure 4.4

The Type 2 Native-API JDBC driver.

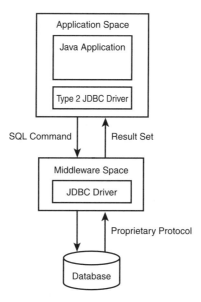

Figure 4.5

The Type 3 JDBC-Net driver.

Type 4: Native-Protocol, Pure Java Driver

The Type 4 drivers are pure Java drivers that communicate directly with the vendor's database. They do this by converting JDBC commands directly into the database engine's native protocol. The Type 4 driver has a very distinct advantage over all the other driver types. It has no additional translation or middleware layers, which improves performance tremendously. Figure 4.6 diagrams the communications of a Type 4 driver.

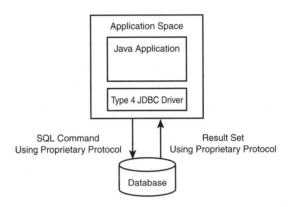

Figure 4.6

The Type 4 native-protocol JDBC driver.

JDBC Basics

Now that we have discussed what the JDBC is and some of its characteristics, let's start learning how to use it. In this section, we are going to discuss how to install and set up a Type 1 driver, make a connection to the database, and perform the basic SQL commands.

Installing and Setting Up a Type 1 Driver

In the JDBC examples throughout this book, we will be connecting to a Microsoft Access database using a Type 1 driver. To install the JDBC-ODBC Bridge, simply download the JDK and follow the installation directions. The JDBC-ODBC Bridge is included in version 1.1 and later.

The JDBC-ODBC Bridge requires no specific setup steps, but the ODBC driver does. For our examples, assume that you are using a PC and running Windows 9*x* or NT. If not, you will need to create your own database using the drivers supplied by your database vendor.

To configure the ODBC data source for the examples, you will follow these steps:

1. Copy to your local drive the database file moviecatalog.mdb, which can be found on this book's Web site.

2. Start the application ODBC Administrator found in the Windows Control Panel. You will see a window similar to the one in Figure 4.7.

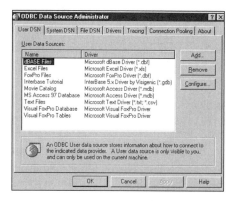

Figure 4.7

The ODBC Administrator.

3. Select the Add button to add a new data source. Figure 4.8 shows the Create New Data Source screen.

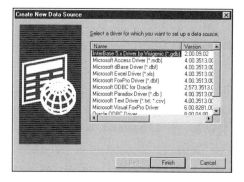

Figure 4.8

The Create New Data Source screen.

4. Select the Microsoft Access Driver and click the Finish button. You will now be presented with the ODBC Microsoft Access Setup screen. Figure 4.9 shows this screen.

Figure 4.9

The ODBC Microsoft Access Setup screen.

5. Enter the string "Movie Catalog" as the data source name and click the database Select button. Enter the path to the location of your moviecatalog.mdb file and click OK. You will now see the ODBC Microsoft Access Setup screen with your changes displayed. Click OK to commit to your changes.
6. You will now see the ODBC Data Source Administrator screen with the Movie Catalog data source in the list. Click the OK button to close this window.

Establishing a Database Connection

The first thing you need to do when using the JDBC is establish a connection to the database. This is a two-step process. You must load the JDBC driver and then make a connection.

Loading a JDBC driver is very simple. It takes only one line of code. In our examples, we will be using the JDBC-ODBC Bridge. The class name for this driver is sun.jdbc.odbc.JdbcOdbcDriver. The following code snippet shows you how to load this driver:

```
Class.forName("sun.jdbc.odbc.JdbcOdbcDriver");
```

When you call the Class.forName() method, it creates an instance of the driver and registers it with the DriverManager. This is all there is to loading a JDBC driver.

After you have the driver loaded, it is easy to make a connection. You make a call to the static method DriverManager.getConnection(), which returns a connection to the database. Its method signature is listed as follows:

```
public static synchronized Connection getConnection(String url,
    String user, String password) throws SQLException
```

The first parameter is the URL that points to our data source. In the case of the JDBC ODBC Bridge, it always begins with jdbc:odbc:DataSourceName, where the DataSourceName is the name of the ODBC data source you set up.

The next two parameters are self-explanatory. They are the username and password associated with the database login. For our example, we will use empty strings for each. Here is the code used to open a connection to our Movie Catalog database:

```
con = DriverManager.getConnection("jdbc:odbc:Movie Catalog",
    "", "");
```

The `Connection` object returned from the `DriverManager` is an open connection to the database. We will be using it to create JDBC statements that pass SQL statements to the database.

Performing the Basic SQL Commands

In this section we are going to look at how to create a JDBC `Statement` object and five JDBC examples that use the `Statement`. In all our examples, we will be using the Movie Catalog database that we configured earlier.

Creating a JDBC Statement Object

To execute any SQL command using a JDBC connection, you must first create a `Statement` object. To create a `Statement`, you need to call the `Connection.createStatement()` method. It returns a JDBC `Statement` that you will use to send your SQL statements to the database. The following code snippet shows how to create a `Statement`:

```
Statement statement = con.createStatement();
```

Creating a Table

The first thing we are going to do is create a database table that represents a list of movie titles. Currently there are two tables in the database: the Categories table and the Types table. Table 4.1 shows the composition of our new Titles table.

Table 4.1   Titles Table Elements

Field Name	Data Type
title_id	INTEGER
title_name	VARCHAR(50)
rating	VARCHAR(5)
price	FLOAT
quantity	INTEGER
type_id	INTEGER
category_id	INTEGER

The application that creates this table can be found in Listing 4.1. Notice that it follows the step-by-step process that I described earlier:

1. Open a connection to the database.
2. Execute a SQL statement.
3. Process the results.
4. Close the connection to the database.

Listing 4.1 CreateTablesApp.java

```java
import java.sql.*;

public class CreateTablesApp {

  public void createTables() {

    Connection con = null;

    try {

      // Load the Driver class file
      Class.forName("sun.jdbc.odbc.JdbcOdbcDriver");

      // Make a connection to the ODBC datasource Movie Catalog
      con = DriverManager.getConnection("jdbc:odbc:Movie Catalog",
        "", "");

      // Create the statement
      Statement statement = con.createStatement();

      // Use the created statement to CREATE the database table
      // Create Titles Table
      statement.executeUpdate("CREATE TABLE Titles " +
        "(title_id INTEGER, title_name VARCHAR(50), " +
        "rating VARCHAR(5), price FLOAT, quantity INTEGER, " +
        "type_id INTEGER, category_id INTEGER)");
    }
    catch (SQLException sqle) {

      System.err.println(sqle.getMessage());
    }
    catch (ClassNotFoundException cnfe) {

      System.err.println(cnfe.getMessage());
    }
    catch (Exception e) {

      System.err.println(e.getMessage());
    }
    finally {

      try {

        if ( con != null ) {
```

```
         // Close the connection no matter what
         con.close();
      }
   }
   catch (SQLException sqle) {

      System.err.println(sqle.getMessage());
   }
 }
}

public static void main(String[] args) {

   CreateTablesApp createTablesApp = new CreateTablesApp();

   createTablesApp.createTables();
 }
}
```

The section we want to focus on is listed here:

```
// Create the statement
Statement statement = con.createStatement();

// Use the created statement to CREATE the database table
// Create Titles Table
statement.executeUpdate("CREATE TABLE Titles " +
  "(title_id INTEGER, title_name VARCHAR(50), " +
  "rating VARCHAR(5), price FLOAT, quantity INTEGER, " +
  "type_id INTEGER, category_id INTEGER)");
```

The first statement executed creates a `Statement` object with the given `Connection`. To perform the actual creation of the table, call the `Statement.executeUpdate()` method, passing it the SQL statement to create the table. Its signature is listed as follows:

```
public int executeUpdate(String sql) throws SQLException
```

This method is used for all update-type transactions. It takes a string representation of an SQL statement and returns an integer. The return value is either a row count for INSERT, UPDATE, and DELETE statements, or 0 for SQL statements that return nothing such as a CREATE.

After we have created the Titles table, the table relationships of our Movie Catalog database will look something like Figure 4.10.

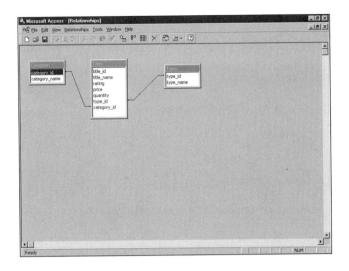

Figure 4.10

The Movie Catalog database.

Inserting Data into a Table

Now that we have all our tables in place, you can put some data into them. Listing 4.2 shows the application used to populate our Movie Catalog database.

Listing 4.2 InsertDataApp.java

```java
import java.sql.*;

public class InsertDataApp {

  public InsertDataApp() {
  }

  public void insertData() {

    Connection con = null;

    try {

      // Load the Driver class file
      Class.forName("sun.jdbc.odbc.JdbcOdbcDriver");

      // Make a connection to the ODBC datasource Movie Catalog
      con = DriverManager.getConnection("jdbc:odbc:Movie Catalog",
        "", "");

      // Create the statement
      Statement statement = con.createStatement();
```

```
// Use the created statement to INSERT DATA into
// the database tables.

// Insert Data into the Types Table
statement.executeUpdate("INSERT INTO Types " +
  "VALUES (0, 'VHS')");

statement.executeUpdate("INSERT INTO Types " +
  "VALUES (1, 'DVD')");

statement.executeUpdate("INSERT INTO Types " +
  "VALUES (2, 'Laserdisc')");

// Insert Data into the Categories Table
statement.executeUpdate("INSERT INTO Categories " +
  "VALUES (0, 'Action Adventure')");

statement.executeUpdate("INSERT INTO Categories " +
  "VALUES (1, 'Comedy')");

statement.executeUpdate("INSERT INTO Categories " +
  "VALUES (2, 'Drama')");

statement.executeUpdate("INSERT INTO Categories " +
  "VALUES (3, 'Western')");

statement.executeUpdate("INSERT INTO Categories " +
  "VALUES (4, 'Sci-Fi')");

statement.executeUpdate("INSERT INTO Categories " +
  "VALUES (5, 'Classics')");

// Insert Data into the Titles Table
statement.executeUpdate("INSERT INTO Titles " +
  "VALUES (0, 'The Adventures of Buckaroo Bonzai', " +
  "'PG', 19.95, 10, 0, 4)");

statement.executeUpdate("INSERT INTO Titles " +
  "VALUES (1, 'Saving Private Ryan', " +
  "'R', 19.95, 12, 1, 0)");

statement.executeUpdate("INSERT INTO Titles " +
  "VALUES (2, 'So I Married An Axe Murderer', " +
  "'PG', 19.95, 15, 1, 1)");

statement.executeUpdate("INSERT INTO Titles " +
```

continues

Listing 4.2   continued

```java
        "VALUES (3, 'Happy Gilmore', " +
        "'PG', 19.95, 9, 1, 1)");

    statement.executeUpdate("INSERT INTO Titles " +
        "VALUES (4, 'High Plains Drifter', " +
        "'PG', 29.95, 10, 2, 3)");

    statement.executeUpdate("INSERT INTO Titles " +
        "VALUES (5, 'Cape Fear', " +
        "'NR', 6.99, 21, 0, 5)");

    statement.executeUpdate("INSERT INTO Titles " +
        "VALUES (6, 'The Last Emperor', " +
        "'PG', 19.95, 12, 1, 2)");
  }
  catch (SQLException sqle) {

    System.err.println(sqle.getMessage());
  }
  catch (ClassNotFoundException cnfe) {

    System.err.println(cnfe.getMessage());
  }
  catch (Exception e) {

    System.err.println(e.getMessage());
  }
  finally {

    try {

      if ( con != null ) {

        // Close the connection no matter what
        con.close();
      }
    }
    catch (SQLException sqle) {

      System.err.println(sqle.getMessage());
    }
  }
}

public static void main(String[] args) {

  InsertDataApp insertDataApp = new InsertDataApp();
```

```
      insertDataApp.insertData();
  }
}
```

The `InsertDataApp` application uses the same `executeUpdate()` method we used to create our tables. We only changed the SQL string that we passed to it, using a basic SQL `INSERT` statement instead. We inserted data into our Types, Categories, and Titles tables, respectively. Also notice that we were able to perform all our inserts using the same `Statement` object. There is nothing preventing you from reusing this object, instead of creating a new one for each execution.

Selecting Data from a Table

The most common SQL statement is the `SELECT`. It gives you the ability to look at the data stored in your tables. In the previous examples, we created and populated the Movie Catalog database. In this example, we are going to look at the data we put in these tables, and we are going to do it with a `SELECT` statement. Listing 4.3 contains the source for this example.

Listing 4.3   `SelectDataApp.java`

```
import java.sql.*;
import java.io.*;

public class SelectDataApp {

  public SelectDataApp() {

  }

  public void selectData() {

    Connection con = null;

    try {

      // Load the Driver class file
      Class.forName("sun.jdbc.odbc.JdbcOdbcDriver");

      // Make a connection to the ODBC datasource Movie Catalog
      con = DriverManager.getConnection("jdbc:odbc:Movie Catalog",
        "", "");

      // Create the statement
      Statement statement = con.createStatement();

      // Use the created statement to SELECT the DATA
      // FROM the Titles Table.
      ResultSet rs = statement.executeQuery("SELECT * " +
```

continues

Listing 4.3   continued

```
        "FROM Titles");

    // Iterate over the ResultSet
    while ( rs.next() ) {

      // get the title_name, which is a String
      System.err.println("Title Name = " + rs.getString("title_name"));
      // get the rating
      System.err.println("Title Rating = " + rs.getString("rating"));
      // get the price
      System.err.println("Title Price = " + rs.getString("price"));
      // get the quantity
      System.err.println("Title Quantity = " + rs.getString("quantity")
        + "\n");
    }
    // Close the ResultSet
    rs.close();
    System.in.read();
  }
  catch (IOException ioe) {

    System.err.println(ioe.getMessage());
  }
  catch (SQLException sqle) {

    System.err.println(sqle.getMessage());
  }
  catch (ClassNotFoundException cnfe) {

    System.err.println(cnfe.getMessage());
  }
  catch (Exception e) {

    System.err.println(e.getMessage());
  }
  finally {

    try {

      if ( con != null ) {

        // Close the connection no matter what
        con.close();
      }
    }
    catch (SQLException sqle) {

      System.err.println(sqle.getMessage());
```

```
      }
    }
  }

  public static void main(String[] args) {

    SelectDataApp selectDataApp = new SelectDataApp();

    selectDataApp.selectData();
  }
}
```

To execute a query, use the same `Statement` object as in previous examples. You just call a different method. The method to perform a query is `executeQuery()`. Its signature is listed here:

```
public ResultSet executeQuery(String sql) throws SQLException
```

It takes a SQL string like the `executeUpdate()` method. The difference from `executeUpdate()` is that `executeQuery()` returns a `ResultSet` object containing the results of the query. In our example, we passed it the string `"SELECT * FROM Titles"`, which returns a collection of rows resulting from the query.

After we have our `ResultSet` object returned from `executeQuery()`, we can iterate over it. The following code snippet shows how our example processes the query results:

```
// Iterate over the ResultSet
while ( rs.next() ) {

  // get the title_name, which is a String
  System.err.println("Title Name = " + rs.getString("title_name"));
  // get the rating
  System.err.println("Title Rating = " + rs.getString("rating"));
  // get the price
  System.err.println("Title Price = " + rs.getString("price"));
  // get the quantity
  System.err.println("Title Quantity = " + rs.getString("quantity")
    + "\n");
}
// Close the ResultSet
rs.close();
```

The first thing you do is call the `ResultSet.next()` method. This method returns a Boolean value, indicating whether the next row in the set is valid. If it is, we can access that row using the `Get` accessors provided by the `ResultSet` object. In our example, we use only the `getString()` method, but they all function the same except for their return type. They take a string value representing the name of the column in the table and return the type that is part of their method name. For example, `getString()` returns a `java.lang.String` and `getInt()` returns an `int`. You can continue iterating over the

ResultSet until next() returns false; at that point you need to close the ResultSet object. When you execute this application, the results will be similar to the following output:

```
Title Name = The Adventures of Buckaroo Bonzai
Title Rating = PG
Title Price = 19.95
Title Quantity = 10

Title Name = Saving Private Ryan
Title Rating = R
Title Price = 19.95
Title Quantity = 12

Title Name = So I Married An Axe Murderer
Title Rating = PG
Title Price = 19.95
Title Quantity = 15

Title Name = Happy Gilmore
Title Rating = PG
Title Price = 19.95
Title Quantity = 9

Title Name = High Plains Drifter
Title Rating = PG
Title Price = 29.95
Title Quantity = 10

Title Name = Cape Fear
Title Rating = NR
Title Price = 6.99
Title Quantity = 21

Title Name = The Last Emperor
Title Rating = PG
Title Price = 19.95
Title Quantity = 12
```

Updating Tables

Another SQL command we need to examine is the UPDATE statement. It looks for a matching condition and makes the specified changes if its WHERE clause is true. An example of this would be if you sold seven copies of *The Last Emperor*. You would need to update its quantity to 5. The example in Listing 4.4 does just that.

Listing 4.4 UpdateDataApp.java
```
import java.sql.*;

public class UpdateDataApp {
```

```java
public UpdateDataApp() {

}

public void updateData() {

  Connection con = null;

  try {

    // Load the Driver class file
    Class.forName("sun.jdbc.odbc.JdbcOdbcDriver");

    // Make a connection to the ODBC datasource Movie Catalog
    con = DriverManager.getConnection("jdbc:odbc:Movie Catalog",
      "", "");

    // Create the statement
    Statement statement = con.createStatement();

    // Use the created statement to UPDATE DATA in
    // the database tables.
    // Update the Quantity of "The Last Emperor"
    statement.executeUpdate("UPDATE Titles " +
      "SET quantity = 5 " +
      "WHERE title_name = 'The Last Emperor'");
  }
  catch (SQLException sqle) {

    System.err.println(sqle.getMessage());
  }
  catch (ClassNotFoundException cnfe) {

    System.err.println(cnfe.getMessage());
  }
  catch (Exception e) {

    System.err.println(e.getMessage());
  }
  finally {

    try {

      if ( con != null ) {

        // Close the connection no matter what
        con.close();
      }
```

continues

Listing 4.4   continued

```
    }
    catch (SQLException sqle) {

      System.err.println(sqle.getMessage());
    }
  }
}

  public static void main(String[] args) {

    UpdateDataApp updateDataApp = new UpdateDataApp();

    updateDataApp.updateData();
  }
}
```

If you examine Listing 4.4's executeUpdate() method, you will see the appropriate SQL string used to perform the previously mentioned update. Run this application and then run the example from Listing 4.3. You will see the change to the quantity value of *The Last Emperor*.

Deleting Data from a Table

The last topic for this section is deleting data from the database. It is not much different from the previous database updating functions, but it does deserve its own section.

To delete a row from a table, you again use the executeUpdate() method. The only change will be the SQL statement you pass to it. In this example, we have decided to take *Cape Fear* off the market. It just doesn't sell as well as it did in previous years. So, we put a SQL string together and substitute it into the executeUpdate() method. The changed call will look something like the following snippet:

```
// Use the created statement to DELETE DATA
// FROM the Titles table.
statement.executeUpdate("DELETE FROM Titles " +
  "WHERE title_name = 'Cape Fear'");
```

After you have run this application, re-run SelectDataApp and you will see that the title *Cape Fear* is no longer in the database.

Using the JDBC in JavaServer Pages

Now that we have covered the basics of using the JDBC, let's look at how you can integrate it into a JSP. It is really very simple. Listing 4.5 contains a sample JSP that performs a query on the previously used Titles table.

Listing 4.5   JDBCExample.jsp

```
<HTML>
<HEAD>
<TITLE>JSP JDBC Example 1</TITLE>
```

```
</HEAD>

<BODY>

<!-- Set the scripting language to java and -->
<!-- import the java.sql package -->
<%@ page language="java" import="java.sql.*" %>

<%

    Connection con = null;

    try {

      // Load the Driver class file
      Class.forName("sun.jdbc.odbc.JdbcOdbcDriver");

      // Make a connection to the ODBC datasource Movie Catalog
      con =
        DriverManager.getConnection("jdbc:odbc:Movie Catalog",
        "", "");

      // Create the statement
      Statement statement = con.createStatement();

      // Use the created statement to SELECT the DATA
      // FROM the Titles Table.
      ResultSet rs = statement.executeQuery("SELECT * " +
        "FROM Titles");

      // Iterate over the ResultSet
%>
<!-- Add an HTML table to format the results -->
<TABLE BORDER="1">
<TR>
<TH>Title</TH><TH>Rating</TH><TH>Price</TH><TH>Quantity</TH>
<%

    while ( rs.next() ) {

      // get the title_name, which is a String
      out.println("<TR>\n<TD>" + rs.getString("title_name")
      + "</TD>");

      // get the rating
      out.println("<TD>" + rs.getString("rating") + "</TD>");
```

continues

Listing 4.5   continued

```
      // get the price
      out.println("<TD>" + rs.getString("price") + "</TD>");

      // get the quantity
      out.println("<TD>" + rs.getString("quantity")
      + "</TD>\n</TR>");
    }
    // Close the ResultSet
    rs.close();
  }
  catch (IOException ioe) {

    out.println(ioe.getMessage());
  }
  catch (SQLException sqle) {

    out.println(sqle.getMessage());
  }
  catch (ClassNotFoundException cnfe) {

    out.println(cnfe.getMessage());
  }
  catch (Exception e) {

    out.println(e.getMessage());
  }
  finally {

    try {

      if ( con != null ) {

        // Close the connection no matter what
        con.close();
      }
    }
    catch (SQLException sqle) {

      out.println(sqle.getMessage());
    }
  }

%>

</BODY>
</HTML>
```

NOTE

A key thing to note is the HTML code that is intermingled throughout the scriptlet code. This is done by closing the scriptlet block with the %> symbol, inserting the HTML code, and then reopening the scriptlet block with the <% symbol. As you look through the generated listing, examine how this is implemented in the _jspService() method.

There is really nothing special about the JSP presented in Listing 4.5. You are simply taking a basic JDBC query and embedding into a JSP scriptlet. When this JSP is first requested, it is compiled into a servlet and the scriptlet code containing the query is placed into the generated _jspService() method. A code snippet follows, containing the generated method, with small changes for readability:

```
public void _jspService(HttpServletRequest request,
        HttpServletResponse response)
        throws IOException, ServletException {

        JspFactory _jspxFactory = null;
        PageContext pageContext = null;
        HttpSession session = null;
        ServletContext application = null;
        ServletConfig config = null;
        JspWriter out = null;
        Object page = this;
        String _value = null;

        try {

                if (_jspx_inited == false) {

                        _jspx_init();
                        _jspx_inited = true;
                }
                _jspxFactory = JspFactory.getDefaultFactory();
                response.setContentType("text/html");
                pageContext = _jspxFactory.getPageContext(this,
                request,                    response, "", true, 8192, true);

                application = pageContext.getServletContext();
                config = pageContext.getServletConfig();
                session = pageContext.getSession();
                out = pageContext.getOut();

                // begin                     out.write("<HTML>\r\n<HEAD>\r\n<TITLE>JSP
                ➥JDBC " +
                  "Example 1</TITLE>\r\n</HEAD>\r\n\r\n<BODY>\r\n\r\n");
                <!-- Set the scripting language to java and -->\r\n
```

```
<!-- import the java.sql package -->\r\n");
// end
// begin
out.write("\r\n\r\n");
// end
// begin [file="D:\\JDBCExample.jsp";
// from=(11,2);to=(33,6)]

Connection con = null;

try {

  // Load the Driver class file
  Class.forName("sun.jdbc.odbc.JdbcOdbcDriver");

  // Make a connection to the ODBC datasource
  con = DriverManager.getConnection(
    "jdbc:odbc:Movie Catalog",
    "", "");

  // Create the statement
  Statement statement = con.createStatement();

 // Use the created statement to SELECT the DATA
  // FROM the Titles Table.
  ResultSet rs = statement.executeQuery("SELECT * " +
  "FROM Titles");

  // Iterate over the ResultSet

  // end
  // begin
  out.write("\r\n<!-- Add an HTML -->\r\n" +
  "<TABLE BORDER=\"1\">\r\n      <TR>\r\n" +
  "<TH>Title</TH><TH>Rating</TH>
  <TH>Price</TH>
  <TH>Quantity</TH>\r\n      ");
  // end
  // begin [file="D:\\JDBCExample.jsp";
  // from=(38,8);to=(89,0)]

  while ( rs.next() ) {

    // get the title_name, which is a String
        out.println("<TR>\n<TD>" +
        rs.getString("title_name") +
        "</TD>");

        // get the rating
```

```
            out.println("<TD>" +
               rs.getString("rating") + "</TD>");

            // get the price
            out.println("<TD>" +
               rs.getString("price") + "</TD>");

            // get the quantity
            out.println("<TD>" +
            rs.getString("quantity") +
            "</TD>\n</TR>");
         }
  // Close the ResultSet
  rs.close();
}
catch (IOException ioe) {

        out.println(ioe.getMessage());
}
catch (SQLException sqle) {

        out.println(sqle.getMessage());
}
catch (ClassNotFoundException cnfe) {

        out.println(cnfe.getMessage());
}
catch (Exception e) {

        out.println(e.getMessage());
}
finally {

        try {

                if ( con != null ) {

                        // Close the con no matter what
                        con.close();
                }
        }
        catch (SQLException sqle) {

                out.println(sqle.getMessage());
        }
}

// end
// begin
```

```
            out.write("\r\n\r\n</BODY>\r\n</HTML>\r\n");
            // end


}
catch (Exception ex) {

        if (out.getBufferSize() != 0)

                out.clear();
                pageContext.handlePageException(ex);
}
finally {

        out.flush();
        jspxFactory.releasePageContext(pageContext);
}
}
```

You will notice as you look through the generated _jspMethod() method that the generated JDBC code is almost verbatim to your JSP scriptlet code. That is really all there is to it. In Chapter 15, "JSP and XML," we will examine a more efficient method of database interaction by incorporating a JDBC connection pool using a JavaBean.

Summary

In this chapter, we covered the basics of the JDBC and its characteristics, saw how to set up a JDBC driver, and examined how you can incorporate the JDBC into a JSP. We also briefly examined how you can break up your scriptlet code by embedding your HTML code into it.

This chapter marks the end of Part I, "Conceptual Reference," which introduces JSP concepts. In Part II, "Techniques Reference," we examine some JSP techniques that really dig into what you have just learned. The next 14 chapters demonstrate how you can put these concepts to practical use.

PART II

TECHNIQUES REFERENCE

CHAPTER 5

Configuring the JSP Server

Tomcat is the flagship product of the Apache Software Foundation's Jakarta Project. It is intended to be a world-class implementation of Sun's Java Servlet SDK 2.2 and JavaServer Pages 1.1 specifications. Tomcat is, at the time of this writing, the only released implementation of both of these specifications. Because of Tomcat's compliance with the latest specifications, it will be the server used throughout this text.

NOTE

The default installation for Tomcat will run under Unix, Windows NT, and Windows 2000. Users with Windows 9x should consult the Tomcat Web site for configuration information.

Installing the Tomcat Server

The first thing you need to do is get a copy of Tomcat from the Jakarta Project's Web site. You can find the necessary links at `http://jakarta.apache.org/`. Figure 5.1 shows the Jakarta Project's homepage.

You can choose to download either class files or source code. For this text we are going to use the zipped class files, so download the file `tomcat.zip`.

Once you have the file decompress it to a local drive. For this text I am installing it to drive `D:`; therefore, my `<SERVER_ROOT>` directory is `D:\tomcat\`.

Figure 5.1

The Jakarta Project's homepage.

The next step is putting your JDK into the Tomcat's classpath. You do this by editing the `<SERVER_ROOT>`/tomcat.bat file and setting the `JAVA_HOME` environment variable to the location of your JDK installation. For my installation I have added the following line to the tomcat.bat file:

```
set JAVA_HOME=D:\jdk1.2.2\
```

You need to make sure this line is added before any references to `JAVA_HOME`. To test your installation, start the Tomcat server by executing the startup.bat file and open your browser to the following URL, substituting your server name:

```
http://server_name:8080/
```

You should now see a screen similar to Figure 5.2.

The next step is to verify the installation of your JDK. You do this by executing one of the JSP examples provided with the Tomcat server. To execute a sample JSP, start from the page shown in Figure 5.2 and choose JSP Examples. You should see a screen similar to Figure 5.3.

Now choose the JSP sample Date and select the Execute link. If everything was installed properly you should see a page similar to Figure 5.4, with a different date of course.

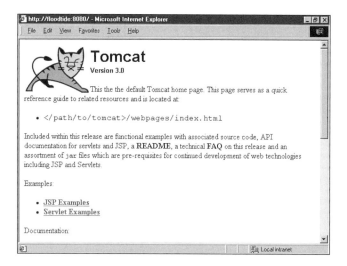

Figure 5.2

The Tomcat default page.

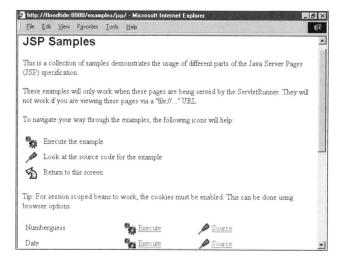

Figure 5.3

JSP Samples page.

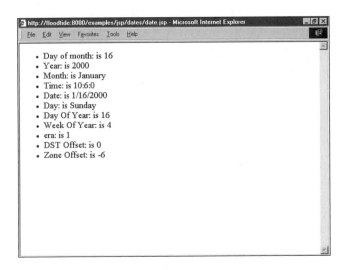

Figure 5.4

The JSP Date page.

If you do not see the previous page, then you need to make sure the location of your JDK matches the location specified, by the `JAVA_HOME` variable, in the `tomcat.bat` file.

Creating the PUREJSP Web Application

With the Java Servlet specification 2.2, the concept of a Web Application was introduced. According to this specification a "Web Application is a collection of servlets, html pages, classes, and other resources that can be bundled and run on multiple containers from multiple vendors." In this text you are going to create the Web Application directory structure, and create a new application entry in the `server.xml` file. Because you will be developing your examples as you progress through the book, we will not deploy our examples into a Web Archive File. If you would like further information about installing Web Applications, which is beyond the scope of this book, refer to the Java Servlet Specification 2.2 Section 9.

The Directory Structure

The first step in creating the PUREJSP Web Application is creating the directory structure of the PUREJSP Web Application. Table 5.1 contains the directories you will need to create. Each one of these directories should be created from the Tomcat `<SERVER_ROOT>`.

Table 5.1   The PUREJSP Web Application Directories

Directory	Description
/purejsp	This is the root directory of the PUREJSP Web Application where we will be installing all of our JSPs and HTML files.
/purejsp/WEB-INF	This directory contains all resources related to the application that are not in the document root of the application. Note that the WEB-INF directory is not part of the public document tree of the application. No file contained in this directory can be served directly to a client.
/purejsp/WEB-INF/classes	This directory is where servlet and utility classes are located.

Adding the PUREJSP Web Application

The final step in setting up the PUREJSP Web Application, which is also our final step in setting up the Tomcat server, is to create a new Web Application entry in the <SERVER_ROOT>/server.xml file. This is the configuration file for the Tomcat server. To add the new entry, add the following section of text directly following the example entry:

```
<Context path="/purejsp" docBase="purejsp"
      defaultSessionTimeOut="30" isWARExpanded="true"
      isWARValidated="false" isInvokerEnabled="true"
      isWorkDirPersistent="false"/>
```

This entry tells the Tomcat server that we have a new Web Application and that it is located in the <SERVER_ROOT>/purejsp/ directory with a document base of purejsp/.

Summary

In this chapter you covered the necessary steps involved in installing and configuring the Tomcat server, including how to add a new Web Application. You should now feel comfortable with what a Web Application is and how to set up a basic configuration.

In Chapter 6, "Handling JSP Errors," we cover how to handle errors in a JSP with an error page.

CHAPTER 6

Handling JSP Errors

Errors can occur in a JSP in two different phases of its life. The first type of error, which occurs during the initial request, is known as a *translation time error*. The second type of JSP error occurs during subsequent requests and is know as a *request time error*. These errors are discussed in the following sections.

JSP Translation Time Errors

The first type of JSP error occurs when a JavaServer Page is first requested and goes through the initial translation from a JSP source file into a corresponding servlet class file. These errors are usually the result of compilation failures and are known as translation time errors. They are reported to the requesting client with an error status code 500 or Server Error and usually contain the reported compilation error. Translation time errors are handled by the JSP engine.

JSP Request Time Errors

The second type of JSP error occurs during request time. These errors are runtime errors that can occur in either the body of the JSP page or in some other object that is called from the body of the JSP page.

Request time errors result in an exception being thrown. These exceptions can be caught and appropriately handled in the body of the calling JSP, which would be the end of the error. Those exceptions that are not caught result in the forwarding of the client request, including the uncaught exception, to the error page specified by the offending JSP. The following sections describe, in detail, how to define and implement JSP error pages.

Creating a JSP Error Page

To create a JSP error page, you need to create a basic JavaServer page and then you need to tell the JSP engine that the page is an error page. You do this by setting its page attribute isErrorPage to true. Listing 6.1 contains a sample error page.

Listing 6.1   errorpage.jsp

```
<html>

<body text="red">

<%@ page isErrorPage="true" %>

<!-- Use the implicit exception object, which holds a reference -->
<!-- to the thrown exception. -->

Error: <%= exception.getMessage() %> has been reported.

</body>
</html>
```

There are two lines of code you need to look at to understand just how easy it is to create a JSP error page. The first is the page directive line, which indicates that this JSP is an error page. This code snippet is

```
<%@ page isErrorPage="true" %>
```

The second line of code designates where the thrown exception is being used. This line is

```
Error: <%= exception.getMessage() %> has been reported.
```

You will notice that it uses the implicit exception object that is part of all JSP error pages. The exception object holds the reference to the unhandled exception that was thrown in the offending JSP.

To get a complete understanding of how the error page works, let's take a look at the servlet code that is generated from the JSP error page. The following code snippet contains the _jspService() method generated from Listing 6.1:

```
public void _jspService(HttpServletRequest request,
  HttpServletResponse  response)
  throws IOException, ServletException {

  JspFactory _jspxFactory = null;
  PageContext pageContext = null;
  HttpSession session = null;
  Throwable exception =
    (Throwable)request.getAttribute("javax.servlet.jsp.jspException");
  ServletContext application = null;
```

```
ServletConfig config = null;
JspWriter out = null;
Object page = this;
String  _value = null;

try {

  if (_jspx_inited == false) {

    _jspx_init();
    _jspx_inited = true;
  }
  _jspxFactory = JspFactory.getDefaultFactory();
  response.setContentType("text/html");
  pageContext = _jspxFactory.getPageContext(this, request, response,
                  "", true, 8192, true);

  application = pageContext.getServletContext();
  config = pageContext.getServletConfig();
  session = pageContext.getSession();
  out = pageContext.getOut();

  // begin
  out.write("<html>\r\n\r\n<body text=\"red\">\r\n\r\n");
  // end
  // begin
  out.write("\r\n\r\n<!-- Use the implicit exception object, " +
  out.write("which holds a reference -->\r\n<!-- to the thrown " +
  out.write("exception. -->\r\n\r\nError: ");
  // end
  // begin [file="D:\\errorpage.jsp";from=(9,10);to=(9,34)]
  out.print( exception.getMessage() );
  // end
  // begin
  out.write(" has been reported. \r\n\r\n</body>\r\n</html>\r\n");
  // end
}
catch (Exception ex) {

  if (out.getBufferSize() != 0)
    out.clear();
  pageContext.handlePageException(ex);
}
finally {

  out.flush();
  _jspxFactory.releasePageContext(pageContext);
}
}
```

NOTE

The generated code included in our examples will differ depending upon the application server used.

You will notice that the _jspService() method looks much like any other generated JSP, except that it has the following lines:

```
Throwable exception =
  (Throwable)request.getAttribute("javax.servlet.jsp.jspException");
```

These two lines make it possible for the error page to access the implicit exception object. It does this by getting the exception object from the request, using the request.getAttribute() method with a key of javax.servlet.jsp.jspException. Now your JSP can do whatever it wants with the received exception. In the next section, we will examine how the exception object gets placed into the request.

Using a JSP Error Page

Now that you know how to create a JSP error page, let's put one to use. It takes only one additional attribute, in your page directive, to make your JSP aware of an error page. You simply need to add the errorPage attribute and set its value equal to the location of your JSP error page. The JSP found in Listing 6.2 uses the error page we created in the previous section.

Listing 6.2   testerror.jsp

```
<%@ page errorPage="errorpage.jsp" %>

<%

  if ( true ) {

    // Just throw an exception
    throw new Exception("A Pure JSP Exception");
  }

%>
```

You will notice in this listing that the first line of code sets the errorPage equal to errorpage.jsp, which is the name of our error page. The rest of our example is just used to throw an exception that will not be caught. That is all there is to it. Just copy both of these JSPs to the <SERVER_ROOT>/purejsp/ directory and open the test-error.jsp page in your browser. You will see a page similar to Figure 6.1.

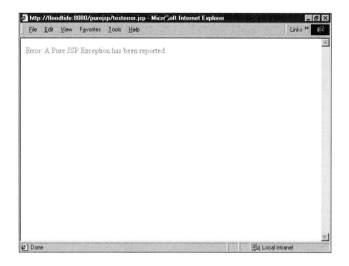

Figure 6.1

Output of the testerror.jsp *example.*

To see how this error is handled in the actual compiled code, let's take a look at the `_jspService()` method generated from the `testerror.jsp` example. The following code snippet contains the generated `_jspService()` method:

```
public void _jspService(HttpServletRequest request,
  HttpServletResponse  response)
  throws IOException, ServletException {

  JspFactory _jspxFactory = null;
  PageContext pageContext = null;
  HttpSession session = null;
  ServletContext application = null;
  ServletConfig config = null;
  JspWriter out = null;
  Object page = this;
  String  _value = null;

  try {

    if (_jspx_inited == false) {

      _jspx_init();
      _jspx_inited = true;
    }
    _jspxFactory = JspFactory.getDefaultFactory();
    response.setContentType("text/html");
```

```
pageContext = _jspxFactory.getPageContext(this, request, response,
    "errorpage.jsp", true, 8192, true);

application = pageContext.getServletContext();
config = pageContext.getServletConfig();
session = pageContext.getSession();
out = pageContext.getOut();

// begin
out.write("\r\n\r\n");
// end
// begin [file="D:\\testerror.jsp";from=(2,2);to=(10,0)]

if ( true ) {

    // Just throw an exception
    throw new Exception("A Pure JSP Exception");
}

// end
// begin
out.write("\r\n");
// end

}
catch (Exception ex) {

  if (out.getBufferSize() != 0)

    out.clear();
    pageContext.handlePageException(ex);
}
finally {

  out.flush();
  _jspxFactory.releasePageContext(pageContext);
}
}
```

The first section of code you need to look at is the call to get the `PageContext` object
from the `JspFactory`, using the `getPageContext()` method. This method obtains an
instance of an implementation dependent `javax.servlet.jsp.PageContext` abstract
class for the calling servlet and currently pending request and response. You will also
notice that one of its parameters is the name we specified as our error page. The following code snippet shows you the call to `getPageContext()`:

```
pageContext = _jspxFactory.getPageContext(this, request, response,
    "errorpage.jsp", true, 8192, true);
```

Now this instance of the `PageContext` object knows to which page to forward all uncaught errors. And this is done in the following code snippet:

```
catch (Exception ex) {

if (out.getBufferSize() != 0)

  out.clear();
  pageContext.handlePageException(ex);
}
```

You can see that this `catch` block catches all uncaught exceptions and passes them to the `pageContext.handlePageException()` method, which in turn places the exception into the request and forwards it to the error page referenced during the creation of the `PageContext`.

Summary

In this chapter, you covered the types of errors that can occur in a JSP. You have also seen how you can handle and respond to these errors, using a JSP error page.

In Chapter 7, "Using the `include` Directive," you are going to take a look at some techniques involved in using the remaining JSP directives.

CHAPTER 7

Using the include Directive

This chapter discusses the JSP `include` directive. We'll talk about how it works and when it is processed.

The include Directive

As we discussed in Chapter 1, "JSP Overview: The Components of a Java Server Page," the JSP `include` directive is used to insert text and code into a JSP at translation time. After the initial request is processed, the data included does not change until the included file is changed and the server is restarted. The syntax of the `include` directive is

```
<%@ include file="relativeURLspec" %>
```

The file that the `file` attribute points to can reference a normal text HTML file or a JSP file, which will be evaluated at translation time.

NOTE

Currently the JSP 1.1 specification does not have a defined method for notifying the JSP engine that the included file has changed.

Example: A Standard Title Bar

One of the more frequent uses for the `include` directive is to easily establish a common look and feel for JSPs. You can do this by creating a standard navigation or title bar in a separate file that will be included in all of your JSPs. To further explain how this works, let's create our own title bar that includes a logo and the name of the user that is logged in. Listing 7.1 contains the JSP file we will be including.

Listing 7.1   titlebar.jsp

```
<table>
  <tr>
    <td>
      <img src="sams.gif">
    </td>
    <td>
      <%
        // Get the User's Name from the session
        out.println("<b>Hello: " + request.getParameter("user") + "</b>");
      %>
    </td>
  </tr>
</table>
```

You can see that this is a simple JSP that creates an HTML table with an image and the name of the user retrieved from the implicit request object. You should copy this file to your *<SERVER_ROOT>*/purejsp/ directory.

Creating the JSP

Now let's create a JSP that will use the titlebar.jsp. To do this you should create a JSP file with an include directive referencing the JSP in Listing 7.1. Listing 7.2 contains an example of how you could do this.

Listing 7.2   welcome.jsp

```
<%@ page errorPage="errorpage.jsp" %>

<html>
  <head>
    <title>Welcome to JSP</title>
  </head>
  <body>
    <table width="100%">
      <tr>
        <td>
          <%@ include file="titlebar.jsp" %>
        </td>
      </tr>
      <tr>
        <td>
        <%
          // Print a simple message in the client area.
          out.println("<center><b>This is the client area.</b></center>");
        %>
        </td>
      </tr>
    </table>
  </body>
</html>
```

There is really only one section of this file that you need to examine. It is the line

```
<%@ include file="titlebar.jsp" %>
```

This line simply evaluates the referenced JSP, `titlebar.jsp`, and embeds the results into the `welcome.jsp`. Copy this file and the image file `sams.gif` to the `<SERVER_ROOT>/purejsp/` directory and then open your browser to the URL

```
http://localhost:8080/purejsp/welcome.jsp?user=Joe
```

The resulting Web page should look similar to Figure 7.1.

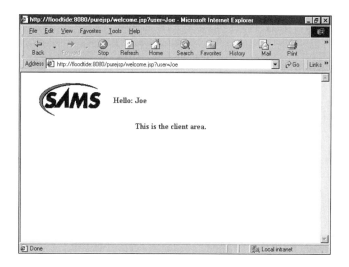

Figure 7.1

Output of the `welcome.jsp` *example.*

As we have in many previous chapters, let's take a look at the generated servlet code to get a better understanding of exactly what is happening. The following code snippet contains the `welcome.jsp`'s `_jspService()` method:

```
public void _jspService(HttpServletRequest request,
  HttpServletResponse  response)
  throws IOException, ServletException {

  JspFactory _jspxFactory = null;
  PageContext pageContext = null;
  HttpSession session = null;
  ServletContext application = null;
  ServletConfig config = null;
  JspWriter out = null;
```

```
Object page = this;
String   _value = null;

try {

  if (_jspx_inited == false) {

    _jspx_init();
    _jspx_inited = true;
  }
  _jspxFactory = JspFactory.getDefaultFactory();
  response.setContentType("text/html");
  pageContext = _jspxFactory.getPageContext(this, request, response,
                  "errorpage.jsp", true, 8192, true);

  application = pageContext.getServletContext();
  config = pageContext.getServletConfig();
  session = pageContext.getSession();
  out = pageContext.getOut();

  // begin
  out.write("\r\n\r\n<html>\r\n  <head>\r\n     " +
    "<title>Welcome to JSP</title>\r\n  </head>\r\n  <body>\r\n    " +
    "<table width=\"100%\">\r\n      <tr>\r\n        <td>\r\n          ");
  // end
  // begin
  out.write("<table>\r\n  <tr>\r\n    <td>\r\n       " +
    "<img src=\"sams.gif\">\r\n    </td>\r\n    <td>\r\n       ");
  // end
  // begin [file="D:\\titlebar.jsp";from=(6,8);to=(9,6)]

  // Get the User's Name from the session
  out.println("<b>Hello: " + request.getParameter("user") + "</b>");

  // end
  // begin
  out.write("\r\n    </td>\r\n  </tr>\r\n</table>   \r\n\r\n      " +
    "</td>\r\n      </tr>\r\n      <tr>\r\n        <td>\r\n          ");
  // end
  // begin [file="D:\\welcome.jsp";from=(15,10);to=(18,8)]

  // Print a simple message in the client area.
  out.println("<center><b>This is the client area.</b></center>");

  // end
  // begin
  out.write("\r\n          </td>\r\n        </tr>\r\n      </table>\r\n   " +
    "</body>\r\n</html>\r\n\r\n");
  // end
```

```
  }
  catch (Exception ex) {

    if (out.getBufferSize() != 0)

      out.clear();
    pageContext.handlePageException(ex);
  }
  finally {

    out.flush();
    _jspxFactory.releasePageContext(pageContext);
  }
}
```

You can see where the titlebar.jsp file is included by the comment reference:

```
// begin [file="D:\\titlebar.jsp";from=(6,8);to=(9,6)]
```

It marks the start of the output generated by the JSP engine during translation. You should also notice that the resulting servlet code is just like the source generated by any other JSP. It is just embedded directly into the _jspService() method of the JSP that included it.

To see the difference between translation and request-time JSP processing, try changing the titlebar.jsp page, while the server is still running, and then reload the welcome.jsp file. You will notice that your changes do not take effect until you restart the server, because they are processed at translation time. This is one of the drawbacks of using the include directive. In Chapter 10, "Using JSP Standard Actions," we will take a look at the standard action <jsp:include>, which overcomes this limitation by processing the include at request time.

Summary

In this chapter, we covered how the JSP include directive works. We also discussed when the include directive is processed. At this point you should know how to include a JSP or HTML file using the include directive and you should also know when included file changes take effect.

In Chapter 8, "JavaServer Pages and Inheritance," we are going to cover how you can extend the functionality of a JSP using inheritance.

CHAPTER 8

JavaServer Pages and Inheritance

Extending a JavaServer page from another servlet or JSP can be a very tricky task. It is also a task that is not recommended by Sun, because in doing so you restrict the capability of the JSP Engine to provide specialized superclasses that might improve the quality of a rendered servlet.

NOTE

Two of the more common reasons to use JSP subclasses are to provide a common look and feel and also to provide a standard set of utility methods. You might want to investigate using includes to satisfy the first reason and utility classes to satisfy the latter.

To extend a JSP from a superclass, your superclass and JSP must satisfy certain requirements.

The Superclass

The requirements for your superclass are as follows:

- It must implement the HttpJspPage, if it uses the HTTP protocol, or JspPage, if it does not.
- All methods from the Servlet interface must be declared final.
- The service() method must invoke the _jspService() method.
- The init() method must invoke the jspInit() method.
- The destroy() method must invoke the jspDestroy() method.

A sample superclass servlet, which provides two utility methods for getting the username and company name, can be found in Listing 8.1.

Listing 8.1   PureJSPBase.java

```java
import javax.servlet.*;
import javax.servlet.http.*;
import javax.servlet.jsp.HttpJspPage;
import java.io.*;
import java.util.*;

public abstract class PureJSPBase
  extends HttpServlet
  implements HttpJspPage {

  private ServletConfig config;

  //Initialize global variables
  final public void init(ServletConfig config)
    throws ServletException {

    this.config = config;
    jspInit();
  }

  // provide accessor to the ServletConfig Object
  final public ServletConfig getServletConfig() {

    return config;
  }

  // Provide a simple service method that calls the generated
  // _jspService method.
  final public void service(HttpServletRequest request,
    HttpServletResponse response)
    throws ServletException, IOException {


    _jspService(request, response);
  }

  // Create an abstract method that will be implemented by the JSP processor
  // in the subclass.
  abstract public void _jspService(HttpServletRequest request,
    HttpServletResponse response)
    throws ServletException, IOException;

  // Provide a destroy method
  final public void destroy() {
```

```
    jspDestroy();
  }

  // provide some utility methods
  public String getUser(HttpServletRequest request) {

    // get the User name from the request
    return (String)request.getParameter("user");
  }

  public String getCompany(HttpServletRequest request) {

    // get the Company name from the request
    return (String)request.getParameter("company");
  }

  public String getServletInfo() {

    return new String("PureJSPBase");
  }
}
```

You can see that the PureJSPBase servlet satisfies the requirements for the superclass. It also provides two utility methods that can be used in the subclass for getting the user's name and company from the request object. Now any servlet that extends the PureJSPBase has access to these convenient methods.

The JSP Subclass

The requirements for your JSP subclass are as follows:

- It must provide a jspInit() method.
- It must provide a jspDestroy() method.

A sample JSP subclass can be found in Listing 8.2.

Listing 8.2   SubclassJSP.jsp

```
<%@ page errorPage="errorpage.jsp" extends="PureJSPBase" %>

<%!

  public void jspInit() {

  }

  public void jspDestroy() {

  }
```

continues

Listing 8.2   SubclassJSP.jsp

```
%>

<html>
  <head>
    <title>Welcome to JSP</title>
  </head>
  <body>
    <%
      out.println("Welcome : " +  getUser(request) + "<br>From : "
        + getCompany(request));
    %>
  </body>
</html>
```

You can see that the `SubclassJSP` provides empty `jspInit()` and `jspDestroy()` life-cycle methods, which satisfy the JSP subclass requirements. It also makes calls to its parent's `getUser()` and `getCompany()` methods.

Now compile the `PureJSPBase` servlet to the `<SERVER_ROOT>/purejsp/WEB-INF/classes` directory and move the `SubclassJSP.jsp` to the `<SERVER_ROOT>/purejsp/` directory. You should then open your browser to

`http://localhost:8080/purejsp/SubclassJSP.jsp?user=Bob&company=Sams`

You should see a page similar to Figure 8.1.

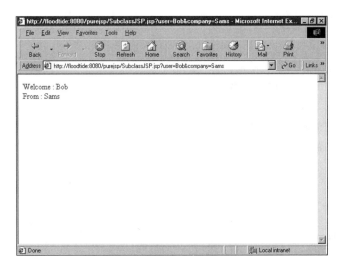

Figure 8.1

The output of `SubclassJSP.jsp`.

Summary

In this chapter, you saw how you can subclass JSPs to provide common utility methods. You also looked at the requirements of both the superclass and the JSP subclass.

In Chapter 9, we are going to cover using the JSP's implicit objects.

CHAPTER 9

Using the JSP's Implicit Objects

As a JSP author, you have access to certain objects that are available for use in JSP documents without being declared first. These objects are parsed by the JSP engine and inserted into the generated servlet as if you defined them yourself.

In reality the JSP engine recognizes the implicit object names and knows that they will be declared by, or passed into, the generated servlet. Here's a example of a code snippet containing a _jspService() method:

```
public void _jspService(HttpServletRequest request,
  HttpServletResponse  response)
  throws IOException, ServletException {

  JspFactory _jspxFactory = null;
  PageContext pageContext = null;
  HttpSession session = null;
  ServletContext application = null;
  ServletConfig config = null;
  JspWriter out = null;
  Object page = this;
  String  _value = null;

  try {

    if (_jspx_inited == false) {

      _jspx_init();
      _jspx_inited = true;
    }
    _jspxFactory = JspFactory.getDefaultFactory();
    response.setContentType("text/html");
```

```
  pageContext = _jspxFactory.getPageContext(this, request, response,
    "errorpage.jsp", true, 8192, true);

  application = pageContext.getServletContext();
  config = pageContext.getServletConfig();
  session = pageContext.getSession();
  out = pageContext.getOut();

  // begin
  out.write("\r\n\r\n\r\n<html>\r\n  <head>\r\n     <title>Hello " +
    "JSP</title>\r\n  </head>\r\n  <body>\r\n      ");
  // end
  // begin [file="D:\\hello.jsp";from=(7,6);to=(10,4)]

  // Print a simple message in the client area.
  out.println("<center><b>Hello!</b></center>");

  // end
  // begin
  out.write("\r\n   </body>\r\n</html>\r\n");
  // end

}
catch (Exception ex) {

  if (out.getBufferSize() != 0)

    out.clear();
  pageContext.handlePageException(ex);
}
finally {

  out.flush();
  _jspxFactory.releasePageContext(pageContext);
}
}
```

As we continue with the rest of this chapter, we will be examining exactly where, in the previous code, each of our implicit objects is declared. We will also look at examples, where applicable, of how you can use each one of these objects.

NOTE

To run these examples, you will need to copy the JSP file from each of the following listings to the *<SERVER_ROOT>*/purejsp/ directory.

request

The implicit object `request` represents the `javax.servlet.http.HttpServlet Request` object that is passed into the generated `_jspService()` method. The `HttpServletRequest` interface defines an object that provides access to HTTP-protocol–specific header information sent by the client. You can see how it is passed in the following code snippet:

```
public void _jspService(HttpServletRequest request,
  HttpServletResponse  response)
  throws IOException, ServletException {
```

One of the more common uses for the `request` object is to access request parameters. You can do this by calling the `request` object's `getParameter()` method, which is inherited from its parent `javax.servlet.ServletRequest`, with the parameter name you are looking for. It will return a string with the value matching the named parameter. An example of this can be found in Listing 9.1.

Listing 9.1   `UseRequest.jsp`

```
<%@ page errorPage="errorpage.jsp" %>

<html>
  <head>
    <title>UseRequest</title>
  </head>
  <body>
    <%
        // Get the User's Name from the request
        out.println("<b>Hello: " + request.getParameter("user") + "</b>");
    %>
  </body>
</html>
```

You can see that this JSP calls the `request.getParameter()` method passing in the parameter `user`. This looks for the key `user` in the parameter list and returns the value, if it is found. Enter the following URL into your browser to see the results from this page:

```
http://localhost:8080/purejsp/UseRequest.jsp?user=Bob
```

After loading this URL, you should see a screen similar to Figure 9.1.

response

The JSP implicit object `response` represents the `javax.servlet.http.HttpServlet Response` object, which defines an object that provides the JSP with the capability to manipulate HTTP-protocol–specific header information and return data to the client. The `request` object is passed into the generated `_jspService()` method. You can see how it is passed in the following code snippet:

```
public void _jspService(HttpServletRequest request,
  HttpServletResponse response)
  throws IOException, ServletException {
```

The most common use for the response object is writing HTML output back to the client browser. You would normally call the response.getWriter() method, but the JSP API abstracts you from this by providing the implicit out object, which will be discussed in a later section of this chapter.

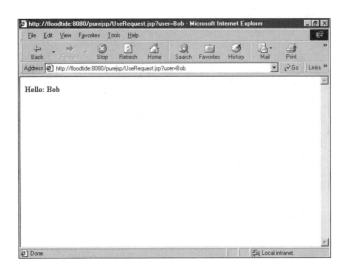

Figure 9.1

Output from UseRequest.jsp.

pageContext

The pageContext object provides access to the namespaces associated with a JSP page. It also provides accessors to several other JSP implicit objects.

An instance of an implementation-dependent pageContext is created by a JSP implementation class at the beginning of the generated servlet's _jspService() method. It is created via an implementation-dependent JspFactory. An example of the pageContext object's creation and its use in the creation of other implicit objects is shown in the following code snippet:

```
pageContext = _jspxFactory.getPageContext(this, request, response,
  "errorpage.jsp", true, 8192, true);

application = pageContext.getServletContext();
config = pageContext.getServletConfig();
session = pageContext.getSession();
out = pageContext.getOut();
```

You can see by examining the previous code snippet that the `pageContext` is used often in the generated servlet. However it is not often used directly in a JavaServer Page. The exception to this is in the creation of custom tags.

session

The implicit `session` object holds a reference to a `javax.servlet.http.HttpSession` object. The `HttpSession` object is used to store objects in between client requests. It provides an almost state-full HTTP interactivity. The `session` object is initialized by a call to the `pageContext.getSession()` method in the generated servlet. The code snippet that initializes the `session` is as follows:

```
session = pageContext.getSession();
```

An example of using the implicit `session` object can be found in Listing 9.2.

Listing 9.2   UseSession.jsp

```
<%@ page errorPage="errorpage.jsp" %>

<html>
  <head>
    <title>UseSession</title>
  </head>
  <body>
    <%
      // Try and get the current count from the session
      Integer count = (Integer)session.getAttribute("COUNT");

      // If COUNT is not found, create it and add it to the session
      if ( count == null ) {

        count = new Integer(1);
        session.setAttribute("COUNT", count);
      }
      else {

        count = new Integer(count.intValue() + 1);
        session.setAttribute("COUNT", count);
      }
      out.println("<b>Hello you have visited this site: "
        + count + " times.</b>");
    %>
  </body>
</html>
```

You should now move this JSP to the `<SERVER_ROOT>`/purejsp directory and open your browser to the following URL:

```
http://localhost:8080/purejsp/UseSession.jsp
```

You should see a page similar to Figure 9.2.

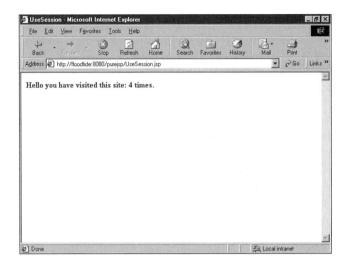

Figure 9.2

Output from UseSession.jsp.

Now go ahead and press your reload button a few times. The count should increment with every reload.

NOTE

> You should also note that the session object has session scope; therefore it will not hold the objects added to it after its expiration.

application

The application object holds a reference to the javax.servlet.ServletContext retrieved from the servlet configuration. The following code snippet, from the JSP's generated servlet, shows how the application object is initialized:

```
pageContext = _jspxFactory.getPageContext(this, request, response,
  "errorpage.jsp", true, 8192, true);

application = pageContext.getServletContext();
```

You can see that the generated servlet simply gets a reference to the current ServletContext and stores it in the application object. The application object has application scope, which means that it is available to all JSPs until the JSP engine is shut down.

The application object is most often used to access environment information. One of the more common pieces of information accessed by the application object is objects that are stored in the ServletContext. These objects are stored there so that they will be available the whole time the servlet engine is running.

The ServletContext is a great place to share objects between JSPs and servlets. In the following example, we use the application object to store and access our application's specific information. We will do this by creating a properties file named Chapter9Prop.txt, as follows:

```
PROP1:VAL1
PROP2:VAL2
PROP3:VAL3
```

You can see that our property file is a simple file with three name:value pairs. Next, we will create a JSP that checks the application for a reference to the Properties object, by calling the application.getAttribute() method with a key that represents the object in the ServletContext. If we do not find the referenced object, we will create it and store the object in the ServletContext using the application.setAttribute() method. Now the Properties object is available to other JSPs and servlets. Listing 9.3 contains this JSP.

Listing 9.3 StoreInApplication.jsp.

```jsp
<%@ page errorPage="errorpage.jsp" %>
<%@ page import="java.util.Properties, java.util.Enumeration" %>
<html>
  <head>
    <title>UseApplication</title>
  </head>
  <body>
    <%

        // Check the application for the shared properties
        Properties props =
          (Properties)application.getAttribute("PROPERTIES");

        if ( props == null ) {

          // If the Properties were not in the application
          // load them and put them in the application
          props = new Properties();
          props.load(new FileInputStream("purejsp/Chapter9Prop.txt"));
          application.setAttribute("PROPERTIES", props);
        }

    %>
  </body>
</html>
```

Now we need to create a servlet that will use the shared Properties object that is stored in the ServletContext. Listing 9.4 contains this JSP.

Listing 9.4 GetFromApplication.jsp

```
<%@ page errorPage="errorpage.jsp" %>
<%@ page import="java.util.Properties, java.util.Enumeration" %>

<html>
  <head>
    <title>Get From Application</title>
  </head>
  <body>
    <%

        // Check the application for the shared properties
        Properties props =
          (Properties)application.getAttribute("PROPERTIES");

        if ( props == null ) {

          out.println("Could not get the Properties from the application!");
        }
        else {

          // The properties were found in the application, iterate over them
          Enumeration enum = props.propertyNames();

          while ( enum.hasMoreElements() ) {

            String name = (String)enum.nextElement();
            out.println("<B>" + name + ":</b>"
              + props.getProperty(name) + "<br>");
          }
        }

    %>
  </body>
</html>
```

As you can see, the GetFromApplication.jsp first checks the application object for a reference to the Properties. If it cannot find the object, it writes a message to the implicit out object stating this. If it does find the Properties object, then GetFromApplication.jsp iterates over the object, printing out the name:value pairs.

Testing the JSPs

To test our JSPs, you need to perform the following steps:

1. Copy all the files into the <*SERVER_ROOT*>/purejsp/ directory.
2. Open your browser to the following URL:
   http://*localhost*:8080/purejsp/StoreInApplication.jsp

3. Then, open your browser to the following URL:

```
http://localhost:8080/purejsp/GetFromApplication.jsp
```

When you open your browser in step 3, you should see a page similar to Figure 9.3.

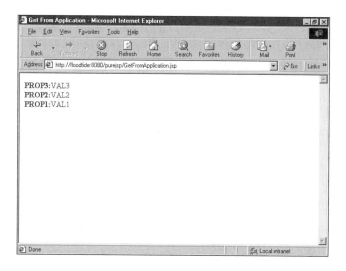

Figure 9.3

Output from GetFromApplication.jsp.

out

The implicit out object is a very simple object that represents a reference to a JspWriter, which is derived from a java.io.Writer. You can see how the out object is initialized in the following code snippet that was pulled from a JSP's generated servlet:

```
JspWriter out = null;
Object page = this;
String  _value = null;

  try {

    if (_jspx_inited == false) {

      _jspx_init();
      _jspx_inited = true;
```

```
    }
    _jspxFactory = JspFactory.getDefaultFactory();
    response.setContentType("text/html");
    pageContext = _jspxFactory.getPageContext(this, request, response,
        "errorpage.jsp", true, 8192, true);

    application = pageContext.getServletContext();
    config = pageContext.getServletConfig();
    session = pageContext.getSession();
    out = pageContext.getOut();
```

You have seen many examples of how the out object is used. It is used to write into the output stream that is delivered back to the client. The most common use is to use the out.println() method, passing it HTML text that will be displayed in the client's browser. Most of your output will be presented to the client in out.println() method. Listing 9.5 contains an example of how you use the implicit out object.

Listing 9.5 UseOut.jsp

```
<%@ page errorPage="errorpage.jsp" %>

<html>
  <head>
    <title>Use Out</title>
  </head>
  <body>
    <%
        // Print a simple message using the implicit out object.
        out.println("<center><b>Hello!</b></center>");
    %>
  </body>
</html>
```

Copy this file to the <SERVER_ROOT>purejsp/ directory and then open your browser to the URL

```
http://localhost:8080/purejsp/UseOut.jsp
```

You should now see a page similar to Figure 9.4.

config

The implicit config object represents the ServletConfig, which defines a servlet-engine–generated object that contains configuration information. The configuration information that this servlet will have access to is the ServletContext object, which describes the context within which the generated servlet will be running. You can see how the config object is initialized in the following code snippet:

```
ServletConfig config = null;
JspWriter out = null;
Object page = this;
```

```
String _value = null;

try {

  if (_jspx_inited == false) {

    _jspx_init();
    _jspx_inited = true;
  }
  _jspxFactory = JspFactory.getDefaultFactory();
  response.setContentType("text/html");
  pageContext = _jspxFactory.getPageContext(this, request, response,
    "errorpage.jsp", true, 8192, true);

  application = pageContext.getServletContext();
  config = pageContext.getServletConfig();
```

Most often, you will not need to use the config object, because you will already have
access to the ServletContext through the implicit application object.

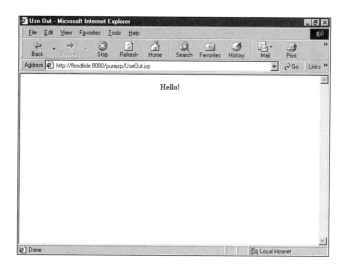

Figure 9.4

Output from UseOut.jsp.

page

The page object is just as it sounds, a reference to the current instance of the JSP. It is
initialized to the actual this reference by the generated servlet. The actual code snippet that does this follows:

```
Object page = this;
```

You use the page object just as you would a this object, to reference the current instance of your generated servlet.

exception

The implicit exception object only exists in a defined errorPage. It holds a reference to the uncaught exception that caused the error page to be invoked. You can find a complete description of the errorPage mechanism, including use of the implicit exception object in Chapter 6, "Handling JSP Errors."

Summary

In this chapter, we covered the JSP implicit objects and how they are commonly used. We also talked about how they were created in the JSP's generated servlet. You should now have a clear understanding of the implicit objects that are available to you and what they represent.

In Chapter 10, we cover using the JSP's standard actions.

CHAPTER 10

Using JSP Standard Actions

The JSP standard actions provide an abstraction that can be used to easily encapsulate common actions. You have already seen the standard actions specific to a JavaBean in Chapter 3, "JavaBeans and JSP Concepts." The remaining standard actions are defined and used, where appropriate, in the following sections.

<jsp:param>

The `<jsp:param>` action is used to provide tag/value pairs of information, by including them as subattributes of the `<jsp:include>`, `<jsp:forward>`, and the `<jsp:plugin>` actions. The syntax of the `<jsp:param>` action is as follows:

```
<jsp:param name="paramName" value="paramValue"/>
```

Table 10.1 contains the attributes and their descriptions for the `<jsp:param>` action.

Table 10.1   The Attributes for the <jsp:param> Action

Attribute	Definition
name	This attribute represents the name of the parameter being referenced.
value	This attribute represents the value of the named parameter.

<jsp:include>

The <jsp:include> action provides a mechanism for including additional static and dynamic resources in the current JSP page. The syntax for this action is as follows:

```
<jsp:include page="urlSpec" flush="true" />
```

and

```
<jsp:include page="urlSpec" flush="true">
    <jsp:param ... />
</jsp:include>
```

The first syntax description does a request-time inclusion, whereas the second contains a list of param subelements that are used to argue the request for the purpose of inclusion. Table 10.2 contains the attributes and their descriptions for the <jsp:include> action.

Table 10.2   The Attributes for the <jsp:include> *Action*

Attribute	Definition
page	This attribute represents the relative URL of the resource to be included.
flush	This attribute represents a mandatory Boolean value stating whether or not the buffer should be flushed. Currently, **true** is the only valid value for this attribute.

To further explain how the <jsp:include> works, we are gong to create two JSPs. The first, which will be the included JSP, will act as the header of the second JSP document. This JSP will search the request for an employee's name and title. Listing 10.1 contains the source for our first JSP.

Listing 10.1   header.jsp

```
<%
  // Get the Employee's Name from the request
  out.println("<b>Employee: </b>" +
    request.getParameter("employee"));
  // Get the Employee's Title from the request
  out.println("<br><b>Title: </b>" +
    request.getParameter("title"));
%>
```

Our second JSP will include the header.jsp in the top row of its table and pass it the employee's name and title, using the <jsp:param> standard action. It will then include some static text indicating the employee's current statistics. Listing 10.2 contains the source code for our second JSP.

Listing 10.2   EmployeeInfo.jsp

```jsp
<%@ page errorPage="errorpage.jsp" %>
<html>
  <head>
    <title>Employee Information</title>
  </head>
  <body>
    <table width="100%" cellspacing="0">
      <tr>
        <td>
          <jsp:include page="header.jsp" flush="true">
            <jsp:param name="employee" value="Bob"/>
            <jsp:param name="title" value="Engineer"/>
          </jsp:include>
        </td>
      </tr>
      <tr bgcolor="lightgrey">
        <td>
          Years of Employment:
        </td>
        <td>
          7
        </td>
      </tr>
      <tr>
        <td>
          Supervisor:
        </td>
        <td>
          Joe
        </td>
      </tr>
      <tr bgcolor="lightgrey">
        <td>
          Salary:
        </td>
        <td>
          $93,000
        </td>
      </tr>
      <tr>
        <td>
          Email:
        </td>
        <td>
          bob@someemailaddress.com
        </td>
      </tr>
    </table>
  </body>
</html>
```

To see the `<jsp:include>` in action, copy both of these JSPs to the `<SERVER_ROOT>`/`purejsp/` directory and open your browser to the following URL:

```
http://localhost:8080/purejsp/EmployeeInfo.jsp
```

You will now see a page similar to Figure 10.1.

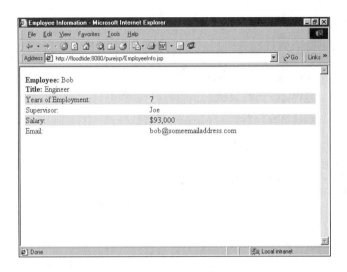

Figure 10.1

The output from `EmployeeInfo.jsp`.

To see how this really works, let's take a look at the generated servlet's `_jspService()` method, which is included in the following code snippet:

```
public void _jspService(HttpServletRequest request,
  HttpServletResponse  response)
  throws IOException, ServletException {

  JspFactory _jspxFactory = null;
  PageContext pageContext = null;
  HttpSession session = null;
  ServletContext application = null;
  ServletConfig config = null;
  JspWriter out = null;
  Object page = this;
  String  _value = null;

  try {

    if (_jspx_inited == false) {

      _jspx_init();
```

```
      _jspx_inited = true;
    }
    _jspxFactory = JspFactory.getDefaultFactory();
    response.setContentType("text/html");
    pageContext = _jspxFactory.getPageContext(this, request, response,
                  "errorpage.jsp", true, 8192, true);

    application = pageContext.getServletContext();
    config = pageContext.getServletConfig();
    session = pageContext.getSession();
    out = pageContext.getOut();

    // begin
    out.write("\r\n\r\n<html>\r\n  <head>\r\n    <title>Employee " +
      "Information</title>\r\n  </head>\r\n  <body>\r\n    " +
      "<table width=\"100%\" cellpadding=\"0\">\r\n      <tr>\r\n" +
      "        <td>\r\n            ");
    // end
    // begin [file="C:\\EmployeeInfo.jsp";from=(10,10);to=(13,24)]
    {
      String _jspx_qStr = "";
      out.flush();
      _jspx_qStr = _jspx_qStr + "?employee=" + "Bob";
      _jspx_qStr = _jspx_qStr + "&title=" + "Engineer";
      pageContext.include("header.jsp" + _jspx_qStr);
    }
    // end
    // begin
    out.write("\r\n        </td>\r\n      </tr>\r\n" +
      "      <tr bgcolor=\"lightgrey\">\r\n        <td>\r\n          " +
      " Years of Employment:\r\n        </td>\r\n        <td>\r\n    " +
      "        7\r\n        </td>\r\n      </tr>\r\n    </table>\r\n  " +
      "</body>\r\n</html>\r\n");
    // end

  }
  catch (Exception ex) {

    if (out.getBufferSize() != 0)

      out.clear();
    pageContext.handlePageException(ex);
  }
  finally {

    out.flush();
    _jspxFactory.releasePageContext(pageContext);
  }
}
```

The `include` is actually taking place in the following code snippet from the `_jspService()` method mentioned earlier:

```
{
  String _jspx_qStr = "";
  out.flush();
  _jspx_qStr = _jspx_qStr + "?employee=" + "Bob";
  _jspx_qStr = _jspx_qStr + "&title=" + "Engineer";
  pageContext.include("header.jsp" + _jspx_qStr);
}
```

You can see that the `String _jspx qStr` is created and then our parameter list, which was created using the `<jsp:param>` standard action, is appended to it. This is what forms our query string that will be passed to our included JSP. When the string is ready, it is passed to the `pageContext.include()` method with the name of the JSP to include. Now the included JSP can parse the passed-in query string.

As you can see, the generated servlet does not directly contain the output from the included JSP. This is because the output is included during request-time. This makes it possible for you to make changes to the included JSP without restarting the JSP engine.

To see this in action, open the included `header.jsp` and make some changes to it. Now reload the `EmployeeInfo.jsp`. Your changes should take effect immediately. This is the difference between the `include` directive and the `<jsp:include>` standard action. To propagate changes using the `include` directive, you would have needed to restart the JSP engine. Using the `<jsp:include>` directive relieves you of this need.

<jsp:forward>

The `<jsp:forward>` action enables the JSP engine to dispatch, at runtime, the current request to a static resource, servlet, or another JSP. The appearance of this action effectively terminates the execution of the current page.

NOTE

A `<jsp:forward>` action can contain `<jsp:param>` subattributes. These subattributes provide values for parameters in the request to be used for forwarding.

The syntax of the `<jsp:forward>` action is as follows:

```
<jsp:forward page="relativeURLspec" />
```

and

```
<jsp:forward page=relativeURLspec">
    <jsp:param .../>
</jsp:forward>
```

Table 10.3 contains the attribute and its description for the `<jsp:forward>` action.

Table 10.3   The Attribute for the <jsp:forward> Action

Attribute	Definition
page	This attribute represents the relative URL of the target of the forward.

The <jsp:forward> standard action is commonly used as a conditional in a JSP. In our example, we are going to get the company id from the request, and, based on it, we will use the <jsp:forward> to go to the employee's particular company page. Listing 10.3 contains the JSP that does this.

Listing 10.3   UseForward.jsp

```
<%@ page errorPage="errorpage.jsp" %>

<html>
  <head>
    <title>Use JSP Forward</title>
  </head>
  <body>
    <%

      if ( (request.getParameter("companyId")).equals("1") ) {

        %>
          <jsp:forward page="SamsHome.jsp">
          <jsp:param name="employee" value="Bob" />
          <jsp:param name="title" value="Senior Engineer" />
          </jsp:forward>
        <%
      }
      else {
        %>
          <jsp:forward page="MCPHome.jsp">
          <jsp:param name="employee" value="Joe" />
          <jsp:param name="title" value="Senior Engineer" />
          </jsp:forward>
        <%
      }
    %>
  </body>
</html>
```

As you can see, the UseForward.jsp simply checks the request for the company id and forwards the user, along with a set of request parameters, to the appropriate company home page. Listings 10.4 and 10.5 contain the source of the company home pages.

Listing 10.4   SamsHome.jsp

```
<table>
  <tr>
    <td>
      <img src="sams.gif">
    </td>
    <td>
      <%
        // Get the Employee's Name from the request
        out.println("<b>Employee: </b>" +
        request.getParameter("employee"));
        // Get the Employee's Title from the request
        out.println("<br><b>Title: </b>" +
        request.getParameter("title"));
      %>
    </td>
  </tr>
</table>
```

Listing 10.5   MCPHome.jsp

```
<table>
  <tr>
    <td>
      <img src="mcplogo.gif">
    </td>
    <td>
      <%
        // Get the Employee's Name from the request
        out.println("<b>Employee: </b>" +
        request.getParameter("employee"));
        // Get the Employee's Title from the request
        out.println("<br><b>Title: </b>" +
        request.getParameter("title"));
      %>
    </td>
  </tr>
</table>
```

After you have copied the JSPs and image files from this chapter's source directory into the *<SERVER_ROOT>*/purejsp/ directory, open your browser to the following URL:

http://*yourserver*:8080/purejsp/UseForward.jsp?companyId=1

You will see an image similar to Figure 10.2.

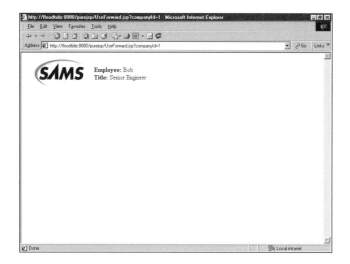

Figure 10.2

The output from UseForward.jsp.

You should also go ahead and change the companyId request parameter to equal something other than 1. This will show you how the JSP forwards based on a conditional.

To see how the `<jsp:forward>` action is implemented, let's take a look at the following code snippet removed from the generated servlet's `_jspService()` method:

```
// begin [file="C:\\UseForward.jsp";from=(7,6);to=(11,8)]

if ( (request.getParameter("companyId")).equals("1") ) {

// end
  // begin [file="C:\\UseForward.jsp";from=(12,10);to=(15,24)]
  if (true) {

    out.clear();
    String _jspx_qfStr = "";
    _jspx_qfStr = _jspx_qfStr + "?employee=" + "Bob";
    _jspx_qfStr = _jspx_qfStr + "&title=" + "Senior Engineer";
    pageContext.forward("SamsHome.jsp" + _jspx_qfStr);
    return;
  }
  // end
  // begin
  out.write("\r\n        ");
  // end
```

```
    // begin [file="C:\\UseForward.jsp";from=(16,10);to=(19,8)]
}
else {

    // end
    // begin
    out.write("\r\n            ");
    // end
    // begin [file="C:\\UseForward.jsp";from=(20,10);to=(23,24)]
    if (true) {

        out.clear();
        String _jspx_qfStr = "";
        _jspx_qfStr = _jspx_qfStr + "?employee=" + "Joe";
        _jspx_qfStr = _jspx_qfStr + "&title=" + "Senior Engineer";
        pageContext.forward("MCPHome.jsp" +  _jspx_qfStr);
        return;
    }
    // end
    // begin
    out.write("\r\n            ");
    // end
    // begin [file="C:\\UseForward.jsp";from=(24,10);to=(26,4)]
}
```

You can see that there is nothing really complicated about this code snippet. It simply decides which JSP to forward to, creates the query string, and calls the pageContext.forward() method with the name of the JSP and the query string.

<jsp:plugin>

The <jsp:plugin> action enables a JSP author to generate HTML that contains the appropriate client-browser–dependent constructs, for example, OBJECT or EMBED, that will result in the download of the Java plug-in and subsequent execution of the specified applet or JavaBeans component.

The <jsp:plugin> tag is replaced by either an <object> or <embed> tag, as appropriate for the requesting user agent, and written to the output stream of the response object. The attributes of the <jsp:plugin> action provide configuration data for the presentation of the element. The syntax of the <jsp:plugin> action is as follows:

```
<jsp:plugin type="pluginType"
    code="classFile"
    codebase="relativeURLpath">

    <jsp:params>

    </jsp:params>
</jsp:plugin>
```

Table 10.4 contains the attributes and their descriptions for the <jsp:plugin> action.

Table 10.4   The Attributes for the <jsp:plugin> Action

Attribute	Definition
type	This attribute represents the type of plug-in to include. An example of this would be an applet.
code	This attribute represents the name of the class that will be executed by the plug-in.
codebase	This attribute references the base or relative path of where the code attribute can be found.

NOTE

There are additional attributes associated with the <jsp:plugin> standard action, but these attributes are beyond the scope of this example. You can find further information in the JSP 1.1 specification.

The <jsp:plugin> attributes indicate the optional parameters that can be passed to the applet or JavaBeans component.

For our example, we are going to use an applet that contains a TextArea object into which a user can type some notes. It does nothing else. Listing 10.6 contains the source for our sample applet.

Listing 10.6   Applet1.java

```
import java.awt.*;
import java.awt.event.*;
import java.applet.*;
import javax.swing.*;

public class Applet1 extends JApplet {

  boolean isStandalone = false;
  TextArea textArea1 = new TextArea();
  GridLayout gridLayout1 = new GridLayout(1,2);

  //Get a parameter value
  public String getParameter(String key, String def) {

    return isStandalone ? System.getProperty(key, def) :
      (getParameter(key) != null ? getParameter(key) : def);
  }

  //Construct the applet
```

continues

Listing 10.6   continued

```
  public Applet1() {

  }

  //Initialize the applet
  public void init() {

    try {

      textArea1.setText("");
      this.setSize(new Dimension(400, 296));
      this.getContentPane().setLayout(gridLayout1);
      this.getContentPane().add(textArea1, null);
    }
    catch(Exception e)  {

      e.printStackTrace();
    }
  }

  //Get Applet information
  public String getAppletInfo() {

    return "Applet Information";
  }

  //Get parameter info
  public String[][] getParameterInfo() {

    return null;
  }

  // static initializer for setting look & feel
  static {

    try {

      UIManager.setLookAndFeel(
        UIManager.getSystemLookAndFeelClassName());
    }
    catch (Exception e) {}
  }
}
```

The JSP source that includes Applet1 is in Listing 10.7.

Listing 10.7   UseJSPPlugin.jsp

```
<table>
  <tr>
    <td>
      <jsp:plugin type="applet" code="Applet1.class"
        codebase="/purejsp/TestApplet"
        width="400"
        height="300">
      </jsp:plugin>
    </td>
  </tr>
</table>
```

The syntax for including an applet plug-in is very similar to including an applet directly in an HTML page. To see the results of this JSP, copy the compiled `Applet1.class` and `dt.jar` files to the `<SERVER_ROOT>`/purejsp/TestApplet directory and copy the `UseJSPPlugin.jsp` file to the `<SERVER_ROOT>`/purejsp directory. Now open your browser to the following URL:

`http://yourserver:8080/purejsp/UseJSPPlugin.jsp`

You will now see an image similar to Figure 10.3.

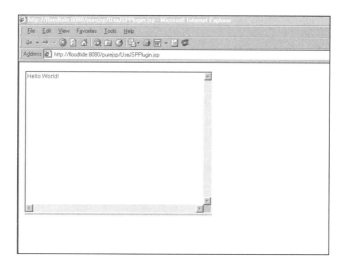

Figure 10.3

The output from `UseJSPPlugin.jsp`.

Summary

In this chapter, we covered the JSP standard actions. You should feel comfortable with how they are implemented and how you can use them.

In Chapter 11, we cover the scope differences when using JavaBeans in a JSP.

CHAPTER 11

JSPs and JavaBean Scope

As we discussed in Chapter 3, "JavaBeans and JSP Concepts," the `<jsp:useBean>` standard action provides four different options for the scope attribute: page, request, session, and application. We will discuss each of these and give an example of how to use them in the following sections.

> **NOTE**
>
> The complete syntax for the `<jsp:useBean>` action can be found in Chapter 3, "JavaBeans and JSP Concepts."

For our examples, we will be using the `Counter` bean from Chapter 3, which acts as a simple Counter. It has a single `int` property, `count`, that holds the current number of times the bean's property has been accessed. It also contains the appropriate methods for getting and setting this property. Listing 11.1 contains the source for this bean.

Listing 11.1   Counter.java

```
import java.io.Serializable;
public class Counter implements Serializable{
  // Initialize the bean on creation
  int count = 0;

  // Parameterless Constructor
  public Counter() {

  }

  // Property Getter
  public int getCount() {

    // Increment the count property, with every request
```

continues

Listing 11.1   continued
```
    count++;
    return this.count;
  }

  // Property Setter
  public void setCount(int count) {

    this.count = count;
  }
}
```

To use this bean you will need to compile it and move the class file to your *<SERVER_ROOT>*/purejsp/WEB-INF/classes/ directory.

page

Beans with page scope are accessible only within the page where they were created. References to an object with page scope will be released when the response is sent back to the client or the request is forwarded to another resource. Objects with page scope are stored in the pageContext. A bean with page scope is most often used for single instance calculations or transactions.

An example of using the Counter bean with page scope can be found in Listing 11.2.

Listing 11.2   PageBean.jsp
```
<%@ page errorPage="errorpage.jsp" %>

<!-- Instantiate the Counter bean with an id of "counter" -->
<jsp:useBean id="counter" scope="page" class="Counter" />

<html>
  <head>
    <title>Page Bean Example</title>
  </head>
  <body>
    <H3>Page Bean Example</H3>
    <center><b>The current count for the counter bean is: </b>
      <%=counter.getCount() %></center>
  </body>
</html>
```

You can see that this JSP simply creates an instance of the Counter bean with an id of "counter". It then prints the current value of the beans count property.

To test the page scope example, move the PageBean.jsp to the *<SERVER_ROOT>*/pure-jsp/ directory and open your browser to the following URL:

```
http://yourserver:8080/purejsp/PageBean.jsp
```

You should see a page similar to Figure 11.1.

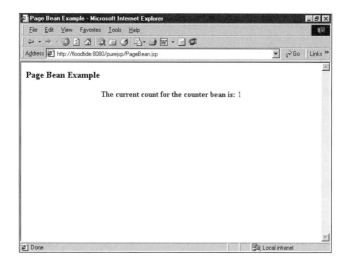

Figure 11.1

The output from `PageBean.jsp`.

You should also go ahead and reload the page a few times. You will notice that the printed count is always reset to 1. This is because each instance of the Counter bean is new every time the page is loaded.

request

Beans with `request` scope are accessible only within pages processing the same request that the object was created in. References to the object will be released after the request is processed completely. If the request is forwarded to another resource in the same runtime, then the object is still in scope. References to objects with `request` scope are stored in the `request` object. Objects that have `request` scope are most often used when you need to share information between resources that is pertinent for the current request only.

For our example of a bean with `request` scope, we create an instance of our Counter bean and forward it to another resource. Listing 11.3 contains the JSP that creates our bean and forwards it to a second JSP.

Listing 11.3 `RequestBean1.jsp`

```
<%@ page errorPage="errorpage.jsp" %>

<!-- Instantiate the Counter bean with an id of "counter" -->
<jsp:useBean id="counter" scope="request" class="Counter" />

<html>
  <head>
    <title>Request Bean Example</title>
```

continues

Listing 11.3   continued
```
  </head>
  <body>
    <!-- call the counter's setCount() method -->
    <!-- so that the current value of the property -->
    <!-- count is changed. -->

    <%
      counter.setCount(10);
    %>

    <jsp:forward page="RequestBean2.jsp" />
  </body>
</html>
```

The only thing you really need to notice about this JSP is the fact that the scope of bean is set to `request`, and the `counter.setCount()` method is called with the value of 10. This is to prove that the JSP to which the request is forwarded is receiving the same instance of the `Counter` bean. Listing 11.4 contains the source for the second JSP.

Listing 11.4   RequestBean2.jsp
```
<%@ page errorPage="errorpage.jsp" %>

<!-- Instantiate the Counter bean with an id of "counter" -->
<jsp:useBean id="counter" scope="request" class="Counter" />

<html>
  <head>
    <title>Request Bean Example 2</title>
  </head>
  <body>
    <H3>Request Bean Example 2</H3>
    <center><b>The current count for the counter bean is: </b>
      <%=counter.getCount() %></center>
  </body>
</html>
```

As you examine the source of our second JSP, you will see that it gets a reference to the `Counter` bean from the request, and then prints the current value of the bean's count property. To see how it works, copy both of these JSPs to the *<SERVER_ROOT>*/purejsp/ directory and open your browser to the following URL:

http://*yourserver*:8080/purejsp/RequestBean1.jsp

You will see a page similar to Figure 11.2.

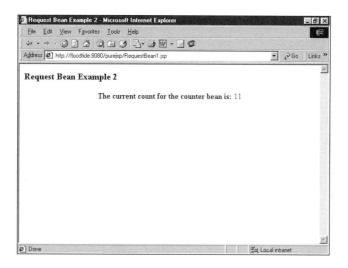

Figure 11.2

The output from RequestBean1.jsp.

You can reload the page several times, but the result will always be the same. The second JSP will print the current value of the count property as 11. This is because the instance of the bean only lasts as long as the request.

session

Beans with session scope are accessible only within pages processing requests that are in the same session as the one in which the bean was created. It is illegal to define an object with session scope from within a page whose page directive has an attribute session=false. References to the session objects are released after their associated sessions expire. Objects with session scope are stored in the session object associated with the page.

Beans that use session scope are most often used when there is a need to share information between requests for a single client. A common application using bean scope is a shopping cart, which we cover in Chapter 13, "JSP and a Shopping Cart." For our example, we use the Counter bean and two almost identical JSPs. Each of the JSPs creates an instance of our bean and prints out the current value of the count property. The two JSPs can be found in Listings 11.5 and 11.6, respectively.

Listing 11.5 SessionBean1.jsp

```
<%@ page errorPage="errorpage.jsp" %>

<!-- Instantiate the Counter bean with an id of "counter" -->
<jsp:useBean id="counter" scope="session" class="Counter" />
```

continues

Listing 11.5   continued

```
<html>
  <head>
    <title>Session Bean Example 1</title>
  </head>
  <body>
    <H3>Session Bean Example 1</H3>
    <center><b>The current count for the counter bean is: </b>
      <%=counter.getCount() %></center>
  </body>
</html>
```

Listing 11.6   SessionBean2.jsp

```
<%@ page errorPage="errorpage.jsp" %>

<!-- Instantiate the Counter bean with an id of "counter" -->
<jsp:useBean id="counter" scope="session" class="Counter" />

<html>
  <head>
    <title>Session Bean Example 2</title>
  </head>
  <body>
    <H3>Session Bean Example 2</H3>
    <center><b>The current count for the counter bean is: </b>
      <%=counter.getCount() %></center>
  </body>
</html>
```

You can see that the only difference between these two JSPs is the values of the HTML <title> and <h3> tags.

To see how a session bean works, copy both of these JSPs to the <SERVER_ROOT>/purejsp/ directory and open your browser to the following URL:

http://yourserver:8080/purejsp/SessionBean1.jsp

You should see an image similar to Figure 11.3.

Go ahead and hit your reload button several times. You should see the count increase each time the page is reloaded. Now use the same browser instance to open the following URL:

http://yourserver:8080/purejsp/SessionBean2.jsp

You will see the count increment from the last count from the first JSP. This is because the Counter bean is stored in the session of the client. Now open a completely new instance of the browser and you will see the value of the count property is reset. This is because each instance of a client creates its own instance of the HttpSession, which is where the Counter bean is stored.

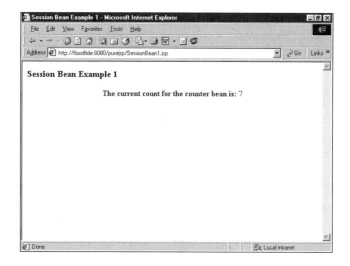

Figure 11.3

The output from SessionBean1.jsp.

application

Beans with application scope are accessible within pages processing requests that are in the same application space as the page in which they were created. References to the object will be released when the runtime environment reclaims the ServletContext. More simply put, this means that, until the JSP engine is restarted, the bean created with application scope will be available. Beans with application scope are best used when you need to share information between JSPs and servlets for the life of your application.

To give an example of application scope, we are going to use two JSPs. The first will load the Counter bean using an id of counter and a scope of application. It will then print out the current value of the Counter bean, using the Counter.getCount() method. Listing 11.7 contains the source for our first JSP.

Listing 11.7 ApplicationBean1.jsp

```
<%@ page errorPage="errorpage.jsp" %>
<!-- Instantiate the Counter bean with an id of "counter" -->
<jsp:useBean id="counter" scope="application" class="Counter" />
<html>
  <head>
    <title>Application Bean Example 1</title>
  </head>
  <body>
    <H3>Application Bean Example 1</H3>
    <center><b>The current count for the counter bean is: </b>
      <%=counter.getCount() %></center>
  </body>
</html>
```

Our second JSP does exactly as the first except that, because both beans have an id of counter and application scope, it will find the bean and not have to create it. Listing 11.8 contains the source for our second JSP.

Listing 11.8 ApplicationBean2.jsp

```
<%@ page errorPage="errorpage.jsp" %>
<!-- Instantiate the Counter bean with an id of "counter" -->
<jsp:useBean id="counter" scope="application" class="Counter" />
<html>
  <head>
    <title>Application Bean Example 2</title>
  </head>
  <body>
    <H3>Application Bean Example 2</H3>
    <center><b>The current count for the counter bean is: </b>
      <%=counter.getCount() %></center>
  </body>
</html>
```

Go ahead and copy both of these JSPs to the <SERVER_ROOT>/purejsp/ directory and open your browser to the following URL:

```
http://yourserver:8080/purejsp/ApplicationBean1.jsp
```

Hit the reload button a few times and watch the count go up. You will see a page similar to Figure 11.4.

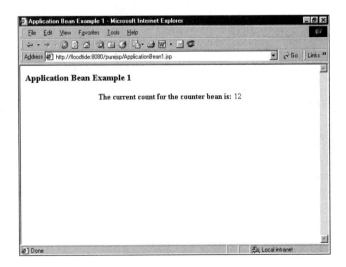

Figure 11.4

The output from ApplicationBean1.jsp.

Now open another browser window to the second JSP using the following URL:

`http://yourserver:8080/purejsp/ApplicationBean2.jsp`

Hit the reload button a few times and watch the count go up. You will see, as each page increments the other page's instance, that both of these pages share the same instance of the `Counter` bean. They will share this instance until the JSP engine is shut down.

Summary

In this chapter, we covered how JSP beans are scoped. You should feel comfortable with the different types of JSP scope. You should also understand how the life of a JSP bean is determined by its scope.

In Chapter 12, we cover how to integrate JSPs and HTML forms.

CHAPTER 12

JSP and HTML Forms

In this chapter we are going to take a look at HTML forms. We are also going to look at how JSPs handle requests from HTML forms.

What Is an HTML Form?

An HTML form is one of the most common ways to gather information from a Web client. It is made up of two basic parts: the <form> tag and the <input> tags. Both of these elements are described below.

The <form> Tag

The <form> tag is what defines the form. It tells the HTML browser how to display the form and how the browser should submit the form. The basic syntax of an HTML <form> tag is listed below:

```
<form method="GET|POST" action="URL">...</form>
```

The <form> tag's attributes are described in Table 12.1.

Table 12.1   The Attributes for the <form> Tag

Attribute	Definition
method="GET|POST"	This attribute determines which request method will be used to transmit the gathered data. The default method is GET.
action="URL"	This attribute defines the target of the form. It can be a CGI application, Java servlet, or JSP.

The differences between the GET and POST requests are very important to understand.

The GET appends form data to a URL in the form of a query string. The data sent in the query string is in the form of tag/value pairs separated by ampersands (&). A sample URL with an appended query string is listed below:

```
http://yourserver/search.jsp?keyword1=PureJSP&keyword2=servlets
```

In this example, our tag/value pairs are listed to the right of the ? character. The ? character is used to separate the URL from the query string when using a GET request. You should note that the data sent using a GET request is visible in the URL. The amount of data you can send in the query string is also limited to 255 bytes.

The POST method passes data in the request headers sent from the client. It can send an unlimited amount of data in the query string and the query string will not be displayed in the URL.

The <input> Tags

The <input> tags are used to capture form data. A basic form is made up of two <input> types. The first are just your basic elements, such as text fields and radio buttons. The second is the Submit button, which actually sends the data to the target URL referenced in the action attribute. The basic syntax of an <input> tag is listed below:

```
<input type="text" name="inputname" value="inputvalue">
```

The equivalent syntax for creating a Submit button is listed below:

```
<input type="Submit" value="Submit">
```

The <input> tag's attributes are described in Table 12.2.

Table 12.2   The Attributes for the <input> Tag

Attribute	Definition
type="text|submit|etc."	This attribute determines which type of input object is being used.
name="inputname"	This attribute represents the tag in the tag/value pair that is sent in the request.
value="inputvalue"	This attribute represents the value in the tag/value pairs sent in the request.

Using a JSP to Create an HTML Form

Creating an HTML form using a JSP is just like creating a form using any other tool. JSP just gives you the ability to create form elements dynamically. An example of this would be to create a form to gather a user's name and shipping address. The dynamic part would be to have a default value for the user's company name, if the user has already logged in. Listing 12.1 contains a sample JSP that builds this type of form.

Listing 12.1   CreateForm.jsp

```
<html>
<head>
  <title>Create A JSP Form</title>
</head>

<body>

  <form action="/purejsp/RetrieveFormData.jsp" method="post">
    <table align="center" cellspacing="2" cellpadding="2" border="1">
      <tr>
        <td colspan="3">

        <b>Company:</b>
        <%
          String company = request.getParameter("company");
          if ( company != null ) {
        %>
            <input type="text"
              name="company"
              value="<%=company %>"
              size="40" maxlength="40">
        <%
          }
          else {
        %>
            <input type="text"
            name="company"
            size="40"
            maxlength="40">
        <%
          }
        %>
        </td>
      <tr>
        <td colspan="3">
          <b>Street:</b>
          <input type="text"
            name="street"
            size="43"
            maxlength="43">
        </td>
      </tr>
      <tr>
        <td>
          <b>City:</b>
          <input type="text"
```

continues

Listing 12.1   continued

```
            name="city"
            size="20"
            maxlength="20">
        </td>
        <td>
          <b>State:</b>
          <input type="text"
          name="state"
          size="2"
          maxlength="2">
        </td>
        <td>
          <b>Zip:</b>
            <input type="text"
            name="zip"
            size="5"
            maxlength="5">
        </td>
      </tr>
      <tr>
        <td>
          <input type="Submit" value="Submit">
        </td>
      </tr>
    </table>
  </form>
</body>
</html>
```

You can see in Listing 12.1 that the only thing differentiating this HTML form from others you may have seen is that it contains a JSP scriptlet section that checks for the existence of the user's company name in the request. If the user name is there, the scriptlet sets the value of the `company` input to the value retrieved from the `request`. To see this in action, copy the JSP to the `<SERVER_ROOT>/purejsp/` directory and open your browser to the following URL:

```
http://yourserver:8080/purejsp/CreateForm.jsp?company=Sams
```

You will see a page similar to Figure 12.1.

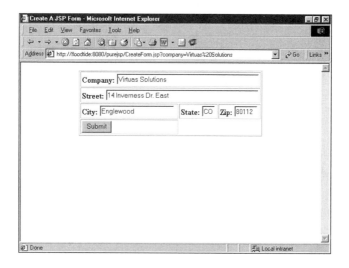

Figure 12.1

The output from CreateForm.jsp.

Retrieving Form Data with a JSP

Now we need to process the data sent from the CreateForm.jsp. To do this we are going to create a bean that has properties that match the tag/value pairs sent in the request. Listing 12.2 contains the source for our Company bean.

Listing 12.2   Company.java

```
/** This bean is used to encapsulate simple
 * company data.
 **/

public class Company {

  private String company = null;
  private String street = null;
  private String city = null;
  private String state = null;
  private String zip = null;

  // Default Constructor
  public Company() {

  }

  // Public Accessors
  public String getCompany() {
```

continues

Listing 12.2   continued

```
    return company;
  }

  public void setCompany(String value) {

    company = value;
  }

  public String getStreet() {

    return street;
  }

  public void setStreet(String value) {

    street = value;
  }

  public String getCity() {

    return city;
  }

  public void setCity(String value) {

    city = value;
  }

  public String getState() {

    return state;
  }

  public void setState(String value) {

    state = value;
  }

  public String getZip() {

    return zip;
  }

  public void setZip(String value) {

    zip = value;
  }
}
```

The source for the JSP used to retrieve the form data is included in Listing 12.3.

Listing 12.3 RetrieveFormData.jsp

```
<%@ page errorPage="errorpage.jsp" %>

<!-- Instantiate the Company bean with an id of "company" -->
<jsp:useBean id="company" scope="request" class="Company" />
<!-- Set the values of the company bean to the request values -->

<jsp:setProperty name="company" property="*" />

<html>
  <head>
    <title>Retrieve Form Data</title>
  </head>
  <body>
  <!-- Output the values of the bean retrieved from the request -->
  <b>Company: </b> <%=company.getCompany() %><br>
  <b>Street: </b> <%=company.getStreet() %><br>
  <b>City: </b> <%=company.getCity() %>
  <b>State: </b> <%=company.getState() %>
  <b>Zip: </b> <%=company.getZip() %>
  </body>
</html>
```

You can see that the first thing this JSP does is create an instance of the company bean, with request scope.

After the bean is created, we set the properties of the bean to the values passed in the request. This is done by using the <jsp:setProperty> standard action. We tell the standard action that we want to use the company bean and set the property attribute to an asterisk (*) character. This tells the <jsp:setProperty> standard action to search the request for parameter names that match the properties of the company bean. If there are any matches, then the standard action will set the bean properties to those values.

To see the results of this JSP, copy it to the <*SERVER_ROOT*>/purejsp/ directory, compile and move the *Company.java*.class to the <SERVER_ROOT>/purejsp/WEB-INF/classes, and press the Submit button on the form created by the CreateForm.jsp. You will see an image similar to Figure 12.2.

NOTE

You can use the request.getParameter() method to retrieve form data if you do not have matching parameters.

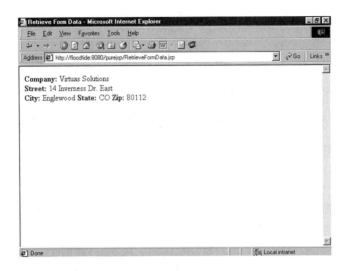

Figure 12.2

The output from `RetrieveFormData.jsp`.

Summary

In this chapter, we covered how you can retrieve form data using JSPs. You should now feel comfortable with retrieving data from forms using either GET or POST requests.

In Chapter 13, we cover how you can incorporate a shopping cart into a JSP.

CHAPTER 13

JSP and a Shopping Cart

One of the more common components used in today's electronic commerce applications are shopping carts. In this chapter, we are going to create a JavaBean that encapsulates a shopping cart, a JSP that displays the contents of the shopping cart, and a JSP that uses the created shopping cart.

Creating a Shopping Cart

The shopping cart we are creating provides transient storage to hold any number of items selected by the user. It provides the functionality to add items, remove items, and change the quantity of an item in the cart. In a normal application you would create an object that would represent a cart item, but for this example we are just adding the properties of an item. Listing 13.1 contains the source for the shopping cart.

Listing 13.1   ShoppingCart.java

```
import java.lang.String;
import java.lang.Integer;
import java.lang.Float;
import java.util.Hashtable;
import java.util.Enumeration;

public class ShoppingCart {

  protected Hashtable items = new Hashtable();

  public ShoppingCart() {

  }

  /**
   * Add a new item to the shopping cart.
   *
```

continues

Listing 13.1   continued

```
 * attributes
 *    itemId - the unique key associated with the item
 *    desc - a text description of the item
 *    price - the unit price for this item
 *    quantity - number of this item to insert into the
 *        shopping cart
 */
public void addItem(String itemId,
  String desc,
  float price,
  int quantity) {

  String[] item = {itemId, desc, Float.toString(price),
  Integer.toString(quantity)};

  if (items.containsKey(itemId)) {

    String[] tmpItem = (String[])items.get(itemId);
    int tmpQuant = Integer.parseInt(tmpItem[3]);
    quantity += tmpQuant;
    tmpItem[3] = Integer.toString(quantity);
  }
  else {

    items.put(itemId, item);
  }
}

/**
 * Remove an item from the shopping cart.
 *
 * attributes
 *    itemId - the unique key associated with the item to be
 *        removed
 */
public void removeItem(String itemId) {

  if (items.containsKey(itemId)) {

    items.remove(itemId);
  }
}

/**
 * Change the quantity of a specific item in the shopping cart.
 * The item must have previously been added to perform this
 * function.
 *
```

```
 * attributes
 *    itemId - unique key for the item to be updated
 *    quantity - the new quantity to be stored in the shopping
 *      cart
 */
public void updateQuantity(String itemId, int quantity) {

  if (items.contains(itemId)) {

    String[] tmpItem = (String[])items.get(itemId);
    tmpItem[3] = Integer.toString(quantity);
  }
}

/**
 * Get an Enumeration to the list of items in the shopping cart.
 */
public Enumeration getEnumeration() {

 return items.elements();
}

/**
 * Get the total cost of all of the items currently in the
 * shopping cart.
 */
public float getCost() {

  Enumeration enum = items.elements();
  String[] tmpItem;
  float totalCost = 0.00f;

  while (enum.hasMoreElements()) {

    tmpItem = (String[])enum.nextElement();
    totalCost += (Integer.parseInt(tmpItem[3]) *
      Float.parseFloat(tmpItem[2]));
  }
  return totalCost;
}

/**
 * Get the total number of items currently in the shopping cart.
 */
public int getNumOfItems() {

  Enumeration enum = items.elements();
  String[] tmpItem;
  int numOfItems = 0;
```

continues

Listing 13.1   continued

```
  while (enum.hasMoreElements()) {

    tmpItem = (String[])enum.nextElement();
    numOfItems += Integer.parseInt(tmpItem[3]);
  }

  return numOfItems;
  }
}
```

To install this bean, compile it and move the resulting class file to the *<SERVER_ROOT>*/purejsp/WEB-INF/classes/ directory.

Integrating the Shopping Cart

Now that we have a shopping cart bean, let's create a JSP that makes use of the cart. The JSP that we have created to do this is in Listing 13.2.

Listing 13.2   AddToShoppingCart.jsp

```
<%@ page errorPage="errorpage.jsp" %>

<!-- Instantiate the ShoppingCart bean with an id of "cart" -->
<jsp:useBean id="cart" scope="session" class="ShoppingCart" />

<html>
  <head>
    <title>DVD Catalog</title>
  </head>
  <body>
  <!-- If there is a new item on the request add it to the cart -->
  <%
    String id = request.getParameter("id");
    if ( id != null ) {

      String desc = request.getParameter("desc");
      Float price = new Float(request.getParameter("price"));

      cart.addItem(id, desc, price.floatValue(), 1);
    }
  %>
  <!-- Print the current quantity of the ShoppingCart -->
  <a href="/purejsp/ShoppingCart.jsp">Shopping Cart Quantity:</a>
    <%=cart.getNumOfItems() %>
  <hr>
  <center><h3>DVD Catalog</h3></center>
  <table border="1" width="300" cellspacing="0"
  cellpadding="2" align="center">
    <tr><th>Description</th><th>Price</th></tr>
<!-- ("123", "First thing added", 123.45f, 4); -->
    <tr>
```

```
        <form action="/purejsp/AddToShoppingCart.jsp" method="post">
          <td>Happy Gilmore</td>
          <td>$19.95</td>
          <td><input type="submit" name="Submit" value="Add"></td>
          <input type="hidden" name="id" value="1">
          <input type="hidden" name="desc" value="Happy Gilmore">
          <input type="hidden" name="price" value="19.95">
        </form>
      </tr>
      <tr>
        <form action="/purejsp/AddToShoppingCart.jsp" method="post">
          <td>Wayne's World</td>
          <td>$19.95</td>
          <td><input type="submit" name="Submit" value="Add"></td>
          <input type="hidden" name="id" value="2">
          <input type="hidden" name="desc" value="Wayne's World">
          <input type="hidden" name="price" value="19.95">
        </form>
      </tr>
      <tr>
        <form action="/purejsp/AddToShoppingCart.jsp" method="post">
          <td>Tommy Boy</td>
          <td>$15.95</td>
          <td><input type="submit" name="Submit" value="Add"></td>
          <input type="hidden" name="id" value="3">
          <input type="hidden" name="desc" value="Tommy Boy">
          <input type="hidden" name="price" value="15.95">
        </form>
      </tr>
      <tr>
        <form action="/purejsp/AddToShoppingCart.jsp" method="post">
          <td>Lethal Weapon 4</td>
          <td>$19.95</td>
          <td><input type="submit" name="Submit" value="Add"></td>
          <input type="hidden" name="id" value="4">
          <input type="hidden" name="desc" value="Lethal Weapon 4">
          <input type="hidden" name="price" value="19.95">
        </form>
      </tr>
      <tr>
        <form action="/purejsp/AddToShoppingCart.jsp" method="post">
          <td>Nutty Professor</td>
          <td>$19.95</td>
          <td><input type="submit" name="Submit" value="Add"></td>
          <input type="hidden" name="id" value="5">
          <input type="hidden" name="desc" value="Nutty Professor">
          <input type="hidden" name="price" value="19.95">
        </form>
      </tr>
      </table>
  </body>
</html>
```

There are four areas of this JSP on which you need to focus. The first is the line of code that instantiates the `ShoppingCart` bean. This is done with the `<jsp:useBean>` standard action. The bean is created with an `id` of `cart` and has `session` scope. The following code snippet contains this action:

```
<jsp:useBean id="cart" scope="session" class="ShoppingCart" />
```

NOTE

> You should notice that the `cart` object has `session` scope. This is the logical place for a shopping cart to be stored. This is because the session is client specific.

The next area you need to examine is the JSP scriptlet section that checks the request for items to add to the shopping cart. If the scriptlet finds any items in the request, it will add them using the `ShoppingCart.add()` method. The code snippet that contains this scriptlet is listed below:

```
<%
  String id = request.getParameter("id");
  if ( id != null ) {

    String desc = request.getParameter("desc");
    Float price = new Float(request.getParameter("price"));

    cart.addItem(id, desc, price.floatValue(), 1);
  }
%>
```

The third section that needs to be looked at is the line that prints the current quantity of the `cart` object. The value is printed in the JSP using a JSP expression. The line of code that does this is in the following code snippet:

```
<b>Shopping Cart Quantity: <%=cart.getNumOfItems() %></b>
```

The final section you need to notice is the form that submits items to be added to the cart. This form references the JSP that contains it. This makes it possible for the previous scriptlet section to get items from the request. To see this JSP in action, copy it to the `<SERVER_ROOT>/purejsp/` directory and open your browser to the following URL:

```
http://yourserver:8080/purejsp/AddToShoppingCart.jsp
```

You will see a page similar to Figure 13.1.

Now add a few items to the cart. You will notice that for every item you add, the quantity of the cart's content is incremented.

Creating a Shopping Cart JSP

Now that you have added several items to the `ShoppingCart`, let's create a JSP that will display the cart's current contents. This JSP will be executed by clicking on the previous JSP's link `Shopping Cart Quantity`. Listing 13.3 contains the source for this JSP.

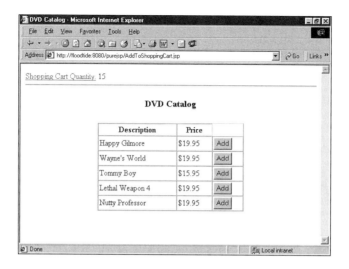

Figure 13.1

The output of AddToShoppingCart.jsp.

Listing 13.3   ShoppingCart.jsp

```
<%@ page errorPage="errorpage.jsp" %>
<%@ page import="java.util.*" %>

<!-- Instantiate the ShoppingCart bean with an id of "cart" -->
<jsp:useBean id="cart" scope="session" class="ShoppingCart" />

<html>
  <head>
    <title>Shopping Cart Contents</title>
  </head>
  <body>
    <center>
    <table width="300" border="1" cellspacing="0"
      cellpadding="2" border="0">
      <caption><b>Shopping Cart Contents</b></caption>
      <tr>
        <th>Description</th>
        <th>Price</th>
        <th>Quantity</th>
      </tr>
  <%
     Enumeration enum = cart.getEnumeration();
     String[] tmpItem;
     // Iterate over the cart
     while (enum.hasMoreElements()) {
```

continues

Listing 13.3   continued

```
        tmpItem = (String[])enum.nextElement();
        %>
        <tr>
          <td><%=tmpItem[1] %></td>
          <td align="center">$<%=tmpItem[2] %></td>
          <td align="center"><%=tmpItem[3] %></td>
        </tr>
        <%
      }
    %>
    </table>
    </center>
    <a href="/purejsp/AddToShoppingCart.jsp">Back to Catalog</a>
  </body>
</html>
```

As you are looking over this JSP, you will notice that a ShoppingCart object is created, or found in the session if it already exists, with an id of cart. The JSP then gets an Enumeration containing the current items in the cart and prints them to an HTML table. That is all there is to it. To see how the ShoppingCart.jsp works, copy it to the <SERVER_ROOT>/purejsp/ directory. After you have used the previous JSP to add items to the cart, click on the Shopping Cart Quantity Link. You will see a page similar to Figure 13.2.

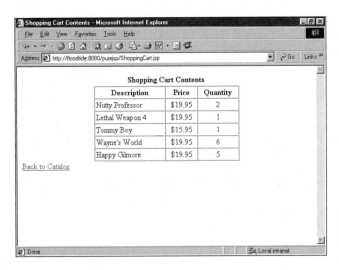

Figure 13.2

The output of ShoppingCart.jsp.

Summary

In this chapter, we covered how to create and use a shopping cart using JSPs.

In Chapter 14, we cover how you can incorporate a JDBC connection pool into a JSP.

CHAPTER 14

JSP and a JDBC Connection Pool Bean

In this chapter, we are going to remedy the inefficiencies that we encountered in Chapter 4, "JDBC and JSP Concepts." Instead of opening a connection to the database with every request, as we did in Chapter 4, we are going to create a pool of connections to the database. This will give us access to a collection of already opened database connections, which will reduce the time it takes to service a request and let us service *n* number of requests at once.

Using a JDBC Connection Pool

There are two classes that we must define in order to create a connection pool: a pooled connection and the connection pool itself. These objects are described in the following sections.

A Pooled JDBC Connection

The `PooledConnection` object simply wraps a JDBC `Connection` object in a class that holds the `Connection` and a flag that determines if the `Connection` is in use or not. This object is shown in Listing 14.1.

Listing 14.1   PooledConnection.java

```
package com.purejsp.connectionpool;

import java.sql.*;

public class PooledConnection {
```

continues

Listing 14.1   continued

```
// Real JDBC Connection
private Connection connection = null;
// boolean flag used to determine if connection is in use
private boolean inuse = false;

// Constructor that takes the passed in JDBC Connection
// and stores it in the connection attribute.
public PooledConnection(Connection value) {

  if ( value != null ) {

    connection = value;
  }
}

// Returns a reference to the JDBC Connection
public Connection getConnection() {

  // get the JDBC Connection
  return connection;
}

// Set the status of the PooledConnection.
public void setInUse(boolean value) {

  inuse = value;
}

// Returns the current status of the PooledConnection.
public boolean inUse() {

  return inuse;
}

// Close the real JDBC Connection
public void close() {

  try {

    connection.close();
  }
  catch (SQLException sqle) {

    System.err.println(sqle.getMessage());
  }
}
}
```

A JDBC Connection Pool

To make use of our pooled connections, we need a `ConnectionPool` object to manage them. The requirements for our `ConnectionPool` object are

1. It must hold n number of open connections.
2. It must be able to determine when a connection is in use.
3. If $n+1$ connections are requested, it must create a new connection and add it to the pool.
4. When we close the pool, all connections must be released.

Now that we know what we want, let's look at what we came up with. The source for our `ConnectionPool` object is in Listing 14.2.

Listing 14.2   ConnectionPool.java

```
package com.purejsp.connectionpool;

import java.sql.*;
import java.util.*;

public class ConnectionPool {

  // JDBC Driver Name
  private String driver = null;
  // URL of database
  private String url = null;
  // Initial number of connections.
  private int size = 0;
  // Username
  private String username = new String("");
  // Password
  private String password = new String("");
  // Vector of JDBC Connections
  private Vector pool = null;

  public ConnectionPool() {

  }

  // Set the value of the JDBC Driver
  public void setDriver(String value) {

    if ( value != null ) {

      driver = value;
    }
  }
```

continues

Listing 14.2   continued

```
// Get the value of the JDBC Driver
public String getDriver() {

  return driver;
}

// Set the URL Pointing to the Datasource
public void setURL(String value ) {

  if ( value != null ) {

    url = value;
  }
}

// Get the URL Pointing to the Datasource
public String getURL() {

  return url;
}

// Set the initial number of connections
public void setSize(int value) {

  if ( value > 1 ) {

    size = value;
  }
}

// Get the initial number of connections
public int getSize() {

  return size;
}

// Set the username
public void setUsername(String value) {

  if ( value != null ) {

    username = value;
  }
}

// Get the username
public String getUserName() {
```

```
    return username;
  }

  // Set the password
  public void setPassword(String value) {

    if ( value != null ) {

      password = value;
    }
  }

  // Get the password
  public String getPassword() {

    return password;
  }

  // Creates and returns a connection
  private Connection createConnection() throws Exception {

    Connection con = null;

    // Create a Connection
    con = DriverManager.getConnection(url,
      username, password);

    return con;
  }

  // Initialize the pool
  public synchronized void initializePool() throws Exception {

    // Check our initial values
    if ( driver == null ) {

      throw new Exception("No Driver Name Specified!");
    }
    if ( url == null ) {

      throw new Exception("No URL Specified!");
    }
    if ( size < 1 ) {

      throw new Exception("Pool size is less than 1!");
    }
```

continues

Listing 14.2   continued

```
// Create the Connections
try {

  // Load the Driver class file
  Class.forName(driver);

  // Create Connections based on the size member
  for ( int x = 0; x < size; x++ ) {

    Connection con = createConnection();

    if ( con != null ) {

      // Create a PooledConnection to encapsulate the
      // real JDBC Connection
      PooledConnection pcon = new PooledConnection(con);
      // Add the Connection to the pool.
      addConnection(pcon);
    }
  }
}
catch (Exception e) {

  System.err.println(e.getMessage());
  throw new Exception(e.getMessage());
}
}

// Adds the PooledConnection to the pool
private void addConnection(PooledConnection value) {

  // If the pool is null, create a new vector
  // with the initial size of "size"
  if ( pool == null ) {

    pool = new Vector(size);
  }
  // Add the PooledConnection Object to the vector
  pool.addElement(value);
}

public synchronized void releaseConnection(Connection con) {

  // find the PooledConnection Object
  for ( int x = 0; x < pool.size(); x++ ) {

    PooledConnection pcon =
```

```
      (PooledConnection)pool.elementAt(x);
    // Check for correct Connection
    if ( pcon.getConnection() == con ) {

      System.err.println("Releasing Connection " + x);
      // Set its inuse attribute to false, which
      // releases it for use
      pcon.setInUse(false);
      break;
    }
  }
}

// Find an available connection
public synchronized Connection getConnection()
  throws Exception {

  PooledConnection pcon = null;

  // find a connection not in use
  for ( int x = 0; x < pool.size(); x++ ) {

    pcon = (PooledConnection)pool.elementAt(x);

    // Check to see if the Connection is in use
    if ( pcon.inUse() == false ) {

      // Mark it as in use
      pcon.setInUse(true);
      // return the JDBC Connection stored in the
      // PooledConnection object
      return pcon.getConnection();
    }
  }

  // Could not find a free connection,
  // create and add a new one
  try {

      // Create a new JDBC Connection
      Connection con = createConnection();
      // Create a new PooledConnection, passing it the JDBC
      // Connection
      pcon = new PooledConnection(con);
      // Mark the connection as in use
      pcon.setInUse(true);
      // Add the new PooledConnection object to the pool
```

continues

Listing 14.2   continued

```
        pool.addElement(pcon);
    }
    catch (Exception e) {

        System.err.println(e.getMessage());
        throw new Exception(e.getMessage());
    }
    // return the new Connection
    return pcon.getConnection();
}

// When shutting down the pool, you need to first empty it.
public synchronized void emptyPool() {

    // Iterate over the entire pool closing the
    // JDBC Connections.
    for ( int x = 0; x < pool.size(); x++ ) {

        System.err.println("Closing JDBC Connection " + x);

        PooledConnection pcon =
            (PooledConnection)pool.elementAt(x);

        // If the PooledConnection is not in use, close it
        if ( pcon.inUse() == false ) {

            pcon.close();
        }
        else {

            // If it is still in use, sleep for 30 seconds and
            // force close.
            try {

                java.lang.Thread.sleep(30000);
                pcon.close();
            }
            catch (InterruptedException ie) {

                System.err.println(ie.getMessage());
            }
        }
    }
}
```

Using the Connection Pool in a JSP

The best way see how the ConnectionPool works is to examine what it does while you learn how to use it. To do this we are going to create a JSP that lists the current contents of Chapter 4's titles table. We will use the moviecatalog.mdb including its ODBC settings. Listing 14.3 contains the source for our JSP.

Listing 14.3   TitlesList.jsp

```
<html>
  <body>
<%@ page errorPage="errorpage.jsp" %>
<%@ page import="java.util.*" %>
<%@ page import="java.sql.*" %>

<!-- Instantiate the ConnectionPool bean with an id of "pool" -->
<jsp:useBean id="pool"
  scope="application"
  class="com.purejsp.connectionpool.ConnectionPool" />

<%

  Connection con = null;

  try {

    // The pool is not initialized
    if ( pool.getDriver() == null ) {

      // initialize the pool
      pool.setDriver("sun.jdbc.odbc.JdbcOdbcDriver");
      pool.setURL("jdbc:odbc:Movie Catalog");
      pool.setSize(5);
      pool.initializePool();
    }

    // Get a connection from the ConnectionPool
    con = pool.getConnection();

    // Create the statement
    Statement statement = con.createStatement();

    // Use the created statement to SELECT the DATA
    // FROM the Titles Table.
    ResultSet rs = statement.executeQuery("SELECT * " +
      "FROM Titles");

    // Iterate over the ResultSet
```

continues

Listing 14.3   continued

```
%>
<!-- Add an HTML table to format the results -->
<center>
<table border="1" cellspacing="0" cellpadding="2"width="500">
  <tr>
    <th>Title</th><th>Rating</th><th>Price</th><th>Quantity</th>
<%

while ( rs.next() ) {

  // get the title_name, which is a String
  out.println("<tr>\n<td>" +
    rs.getString("title_name") + "</td>");

  // get the rating
  out.println("<td align=\"center\">" +
    rs.getString("rating") + "</td>");

  // get the price
  out.println("<td align=\"center\">" +
    rs.getString("price") + "</td>");

  // get the quantity
  out.println("<td align=\"center\">" +
    rs.getString("quantity") + "</td>\n</tr>");
}
// Close the ResultSet
rs.close();
out.println("</table></center>");
}
catch (IOException ioe) {

  out.println(ioe.getMessage());
}
catch (SQLException sqle) {

  out.println(sqle.getMessage());
}
catch (ClassNotFoundException cnfe) {

  out.println(cnfe.getMessage());
}
catch (Exception e) {

  out.println(e.getMessage());
}
finally {
```

```
    try {

      if ( con != null ) {

        // release the connection no matter what
        pool.releaseConnection(con);
      }
    }
    catch (Exception e) {

      out.println(e.getMessage());
    }
  }
%>
  </body>
</html>
```

There are four sections of this JSP that need to be examined in order to understand how the ConnectionPool works. The first section is included in the following code snippet:

```
<!-- Instantiate the ConnectionPool bean with an id of "pool" -->
<jsp:useBean id="pool"
  scope="application"
  class="com.purejsp.connectionpool.ConnectionPool" />
```

This section of code tries to find an instance of a ConnectionPool with application scope and an id of pool. If it cannot find an instance of the pool, it will create one. This bean uses application scope, because the application beans can be accessed by any JSP until the JSP engine is shut down.

The next section of code to be studied is contained in the following code snippet:

```
// The pool is not initialized
if ( pool.getDriver() == null ) {

  // initialize the pool
  pool.setDriver("sun.jdbc.odbc.JdbcOdbcDriver");
  pool.setURL("jdbc:odbc:Movie Catalog");
  pool.setSize(5);
  pool.initializePool();
}
```

In this code snippet we are checking to see if the pool has been initialized. If it has not, then we set the appropriate properties to initialize the pool.

The third section of code to be looked at is

```
// Get a connection from the ConnectionPool
con = pool.getConnection();
```

This section gets a normal JDBC `Connection` object from the pool. At this point the JSP can use this connection just like any other.

The final section to be examined is

```
finally {

  try {

    if ( con != null ) {

      // release the connection no matter what
      pool.releaseConnection(con);
    }
  }
  catch (Exception e) {

    out.println(e.getMessage());
  }
}
```

This final section is used to put our connection back into the `ConnectionPool` for further use. The connection is released by calling the `pool.releaseConnection()` method with the `Connection` object. This method call is placed in the `finally` block to guarantee its execution.

To see how the `ConnectionPool` improves performance, compile the `ConnectionPool` and `PooledConnection` objects and move them to the `<SERVER_ROOT>/purejsp/WEB-INF/classes/com/purejsp/connectionpool/` directory. Then move the `JDBCPooledExample.jsp` to the `<SERVER_ROOT>/purejsp/` directory and open your browser to the following URL:

`http://yourserver:8080/purejsp/JDBCExample.jsp`

You will now see a page similar to Figure 14.1.

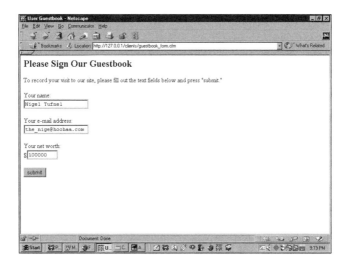

Figure 14.1

Output of the JDBCPooledExample.jsp.

Summary

In this chapter, we covered how to use a JDBC connection pool in a JSP. We also covered how to share the pool with other JSPs, by creating it with a scope of application.

In Chapter 15, we cover how you can combine XML and JSPs.

CHAPTER 15

JSP and XML

The Extensible Markup Language, or XML, is a meta language for creating markup languages used to describe structured data. XML is a self-describing language, composed of tags and values. It is often used to describe objects that are passed in messages between applications. An example of a simple XML document is included in Listing 15.1.

Listing 15.1   item.xml

```
<?xml version="1.0"?>

<ITEM>
  <ID>33445</ID>
  <DESCRIPTION>Austin Powers The International Man of
Mystery</DESCRIPTION>
  <PRICE>19.95</PRICE>
  <QUANTITY>56</QUANTITY>
</ITEM>
```

The first line of this snippet describes a processing instruction which states that this XML document is based on version 1 of the XML specification. Processing instructions begin with a less-than sign and a question mark (<?) and end with a ques­tion mark and a greater than sign (?>).

The rest of this document describes an ITEM object with four attributes: ID, DESCRIPTION, PRICE, and QUANTITY. Each of these attributes is contained in an open *<TAG>* and closed *</TAG>* pair. You should notice how the hierarchy of the object is described in a container-like fashion, wherein the attributes of the ITEM are between the ITEM's open and closing tags. This shows the parent/child relationship of the ITEM object. All XML documents can be viewed as navigable tree structures. Figure 15.1 shows the standard structure of our XML document.

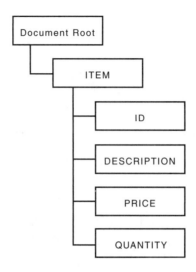

Figure 15.1

The XML document tree structure.

While this is hardly a complete definition of XML, which is well beyond the scope of this book, it is complete enough to show how XML and JSP can be used together.

XML and Java

Now that you understand XML basics, let's take a look at how we can use XML and Java together. There have been many Java parsers developed to interact with XML documents. The three most common have been developed by Sun Microsystems, IBM, and Microsoft. For our example, we will be using Sun's Java API for XML parsing, which can be downloaded from the following URL:

```
http://java.sun.com/xml/download.html
```

Follow the installation instructions for your platform, including adding the jaxp.jar and the parser.jar files to your classpath.

Sun's API is composed of two core components, the Document Object Model (DOM) and the Simple API for XML (SAX API). The DOM is a tree-based API, and the SAX is an event-based API. For our examples, we will be using the SAX API.

The SAX API

As we stated earlier, the SAX API is an event-based API. This means that, as the parser parses the XML document, it triggers certain events based upon encountered elements of the document. To see exactly how this works, let's take a look at Listing 15.2.

Listing 15.2   XMLTest.java

```java
import java.io.*;
import java.util.Hashtable;
import java.util.Enumeration;

import org.w3c.dom.*;
import org.xml.sax.*;
import javax.xml.parsers.SAXParserFactory;
import javax.xml.parsers.SAXParser;

public class XMLTest {

  public static void main (String argv []) throws IOException {

    // Check for the appropriate usage
    if ( argv.length != 1 ) {
      System.err.println ("USAGE: java XMLTest filename");
      System.exit(1);
    }

    try {

      // Get the path to the file
      String xmlResource = "file:" +
        new File(argv[0]).getAbsolutePath();

      Parser parser;
      // Get an instance of the SAXParserFactory
      SAXParserFactory spf = SAXParserFactory.newInstance();
      // Get a SAXParser instance from the factory
      SAXParser sp = spf.newSAXParser();

      // Create an instance of our HandlerBase
      SAXHandler handler = new SAXHandler();

      // Set the Document handler to call our SAXHandler when
      // SAX event occurs while parsing our XMLResource
      sp.parse(xmlResource, handler);
      // After the resource has been parsed get the resulting table
      Hashtable cfgTable = handler.getTable();

      // Print the config settings that we are interested in.
      System.out.println("ID == " +
        (String)cfgTable.get(new String("ID")));
      System.out.println("DESCRIPTION == " +
        (String)cfgTable.get(new String("DESCRIPTION")));
```

continues

Listing 15.2 continued

```
    System.out.println("PRICE == " +
      (String)cfgTable.get(new String("PRICE")));
    System.out.println("QUANTITY == " +
      (String)cfgTable.get(new String("QUANTITY")));
  }
  catch (Exception e) {

    e.printStackTrace();
  }
  System.exit(0);
 }
}
```

As you look over this document, you can see that its main function is to take an XML file from the command line, parse it, and print out the elements that we are looking for. The first thing you should notice is the following section:

```
Parser parser;
// Get an instance of the SAXParserFactory
SAXParserFactory spf = SAXParserFactory.newInstance();
// Get a SAXParser instance from the factory
SAXParser sp = spf.newSAXParser();
```

In this section, we are creating a reference to a `Parser` that will be used to actually parse the XML document. To do this we use the static factory method `SAXParserFactory.newInstance()`, which obtains a new instance of a `SAXParserFactory`. Once we have an instance of a `SAXParserFactory`, we create a new `SAXParser`, by calling the `SAXParserFactory.newSAXParser()` method. The `SAXParser` defines the API that wraps an `org.xml.sax.Parser` implementation class. By using this class an application can parse content using the SAX API.

The next section we need to examine is

```
// Create an instance of our HandlerBase
SAXHandler handler = new SAXHandler();
```

This section of code creates an instance of our event handler `SAXHandler`. To capture events invoked by the parser, you need to either create a class that implements the `org.xml.sax.DocumentHandler` interface or extend the class `org.xml.sax.HandlerBase`, which implements default handlers defined by the `DocumentHandler` interface. For our example, we have extended `HandlerBase` so we only have to implement the methods we are interested in handling. This is much like the event handlers of the AWT.

Once we have an instance of our event handler, we can start the parser. The snippet for this is

```
// Set the Document handler to call our SAXHandler when
// SAX event occurs while parsing our XMLResource
sp.parse(xmlResource, handler);
```

The SAXParser.parse() method takes an InputSource that contains an XML stream and a reference to our handler. As the parser parses our XML document, it will trigger events that will be handled by our SAXHandler, which can be found in Listing 15.3.

Listing 15.3   SAXHandler.java

```java
import java.io.*;
import java.util.Hashtable;

import org.xml.sax.*;

public class SAXHandler extends HandlerBase {

  private Hashtable table = new Hashtable();
  private String currentElement = null;
  private String currentValue = null;

  // Simple Accessor for the Hashtable of parsed values
  public void setTable(Hashtable table) {

    this.table = table;
  }

  // Simple Accessor for the Hashtable of parsed values
  public Hashtable getTable() {

    return table;
  }

  // Called when a new element is encountered
  public void startElement(String tag, AttributeList attrs)
    throws SAXException {

    // hold onto the new element tag, that will be placed in
    // our Hashtable when matching character data is encountered.
      currentElement = tag;
  }

  // Called when character data is found inside an element
  public void characters(char[] ch, int start, int length)
    throws SAXException {

    // create a String containing the characters
    // found in the element
    currentValue = new String(ch, start, length);
  }

  // Called when the end of element is encountered
  public void endElement(String name) throws SAXException {
```

continues

Listing 15.2   continued

```
    // Make sure we have a matching closing element
    if ( currentElement.equals(name) ) {

        // Put the element/value pair into the Hashtable
        table.put(currentElement, currentValue);
    }
  }
}
```

As you look over our handler, you will notice that there are only five methods, two of which are only accessors to a Hashtable. The other three methods represent the events we are interested in responding to. Each of these methods will be discussed in the following sections. The first method we have overridden is startElement(), which is shown here:

```
// Called when a new element is encountered
public void startElement(String tag, AttributeList attrs)
   throws SAXException {

   // hold onto the new element tag, that will be placed in
   // our Hashtable when matching character data is encountered.
   currentElement = tag;
}
```

This method is called whenever the parser encounters a new element in the XML document. A new element would be a starting tag similar to <ID>. When our overridden method is called, we simply hold onto the passed-in tag representing the element name.

The next method we override is the characters() method. Our overridden method is shown here:

```
// Called when character data is found inside an element
public void characters(char[] ch, int start, int length)
   throws SAXException {

   // create a String containing the characters
   // found in the element
   currentValue = new String(ch, start, length);
}
```

This method is invoked when the parser encounters character data inside an element. An example of this would be the value 33445 found in the element <ID>33445</ID>. When our overridden method is called, we create a String from the character array and hold onto the String for later use.

The last method we override from the HandlerBase class is the endElement() method, which is included in the following code snippet:

```
// Called when the end of element is encountered
public void endElement(String name) throws SAXException {

  // Make sure we have a matching closing element
  if ( currentElement.equals(name) ) {

    // Put the element/value pair into the Hashtable
    table.put(currentElement, currentValue);
  }
}
```

The endElement() method is the final event handler that we are concerned with. It is called whenever the end of an element is encountered. If we use the same example from the startElement() method, then endElement() would be invoked when the </ID> tag was encountered. Our overridden endElement() method takes the passed-in name and compares it with the current element being processed. If they match, then the endElement() method puts the element and its character data into the Hashtable.

Now that you understand what happens as each event is triggered, we should get back to our XMLTest application. The remainder of our application is listed in the following code snippet:

```
// After the resource has been parsed get the resulting table
Hashtable cfgTable = handler.getTable();

// Print the config settings that we are interested in.
System.out.println("ID == " +
  (String)cfgTable.get(new String("ID")));
System.out.println("DESCRIPTION == " +
  (String)cfgTable.get(new String("DESCRIPTION")));
System.out.println("PRICE == " +
  (String)cfgTable.get(new String("PRICE")));
System.out.println("QUANTITY == " +
  (String)cfgTable.get(new String("QUANTITY")));
```

As you can see after the parser is finished parsing, the application calls our handler's getTable() method. This method returns a Hashtable containing the elements and their text data that was parsed from the XML file. The final steps we perform are just printing the elements we are interested in from the parsed file. To see this in action, compile and build the handler and application and then execute the application with the XML file we described earlier. Your command line should be similar to the following:

```
java XMLTest item.xml
```

The output should look similar to the following:

```
ID == 33445
DESCRIPTION == Austin Powers The International Man of Mystery
PRICE == 19.95
QUANTITY == 56
```

Using XML in a JSP

Now let's take the previous example and incorporate it into a JSP. Listing 15.4 contains our JSP example.

Listing 15.4   XMLExample.jsp

```
<html>
<head>
<title>JSP XML Example </title>
</head>

<body>

<%@ page import="java.io.*" %>
<%@ page import="java.util.Hashtable" %>
<%@ page import="org.w3c.dom.*" %>
<%@ page import="org.xml.sax.*" %>
<%@ page import="javax.xml.parsers.SAXParserFactory" %>
<%@ page import="javax.xml.parsers.SAXParser" %>
<%@ page import="SAXHandler" %>

<%

    // Get the path to the file
    File file = new File("purejsp/item.xml");
    FileReader reader = new FileReader(file);

    Parser parser;
    // Get an instance of the SAXParserFactory
    SAXParserFactory spf = SAXParserFactory.newInstance();
    // Get a SAXParser instance from the factory
    SAXParser sp = spf.newSAXParser();

    // Create an instance of our HandlerBase
    SAXHandler handler = new SAXHandler();

    // Set the Document handler to call our SAXHandler when
    // SAX event occurs while parsing our XMLResource
    sp.parse(new InputSource(reader), handler);
    // After the resource has been parsed get the resulting table
    Hashtable cfgTable = handler.getTable();

%>
  <table align="center" width="600">
  <caption>XML Item</caption>
<%
  // Print the config settings that we are interested in.
  out.println("<tr><td align=\"left\">ID</td>" +
    "<td align=\"center\">" +
```

```
      (String)cfgTable.get(new String("ID")) + "</td></tr>");
  out.println("<tr><td align=\"left\">DESCRIPTION</td>" +
    "<td align=\"center\">" +
    (String)cfgTable.get(new String("DESCRIPTION")) + "</td></tr>");
  out.println("<tr><td align=\"left\">PRICE</td>" +
    "<td align=\"center\">" +
    (String)cfgTable.get(new String("PRICE")) + "</td></tr>");
  System.out.println("<tr><td align=\"left\">QUANTITY</td>" +
    "<td align=\"center\">" +
    (String)cfgTable.get(new String("QUANTITY")) + "</td></tr>");
%>
  </table>
</body>
</html>
```

As you can see, there is really very little difference in the application code and the JSP code. The only noticeable differences are the way we load the XMLResource and the way we output the results. To see this JSP run, you will need to copy the SAXHandler class file to the <SERVER_ROOT>/purejsp/WEB-INF/classes/ directory, and the item.xml and the XMLExample.jsp to the <SERVER_ROOT>purejsp/ directory. Then load the following URL into your browser:

```
http://yourserver:8080/purejsp/XMLExample.jsp
```

You should see a page similar to Figure 15.2.

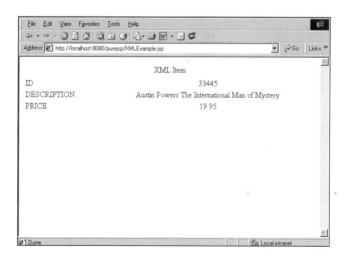

Figure 15.2

Output from XMLExample.jsp.

Summary

In this chapter, we covered the basics of XML. We covered how to use Sun's SAX parser. We also look at an example of how you would incorporate XML and JSPs.

In Chapter 16, "JSP Communication with Servlets," you learn how you can use JSPs and servlets using the Model-View-Controller design pattern.

CHAPTER 16

JSP Communication with Servlets

In this chapter we are going to discuss how you can incorporate servlets and JSPs using the Model-View-Controller design pattern (MVC). The MVC originated from Smalltalk and was used to design user interfaces, wherein the application was made up of three classes: a *Model*, a *View*, and a *Controller*. Each of these classes is defined in Table 16.1.

Table 16.1   The Classes of the MVC

Class	Definition
Model	The *Model* represents the data or application object. It is what is being manipulated and presented to the user.
View	The *View* is the screen representation of the Model. It is the object that presents the current state of the *Model*.
Controller	The *Controller* defines the way the user interface reacts to the user's input. The *Controller* is the object that manipulates the *Model*.

The major benefit of using the MVC design pattern is that it separates the *Views* and *Models*. This makes it possible to create or change *Views* without having to change the *Model*. It also allows a *Model* to be represented by multiple *Views*.

A Servlet-Only Application Model

While servlets are a very sound technology and are excellent for server-side processing, they do have some drawbacks when used alone. Two of the most common of these drawbacks are

- Servlets require an advanced level of Java understanding that HTML programmers usually do not have.
- Servlets generally require recompilation in order to change the client presentation layer.

If we consider these servlet drawbacks, we can determine that one of the greatest strengths of servlets is their server-side processing capability.

A JSP-Only Solution

JavaServer Pages are also a very solid technology. Because JSPs are an extension of servlets, you can do just about anything with a JSP that you can with a servlet. As we have been discussing throughout this text, one of the JSP's greatest strengths is its capability to separate content from presentation. The main drawback with a JSP-only application model is that, as your application becomes more complicated, so does your scriptlet code. This results in confusing and difficult-to-maintain JSPs. If you plan on letting your HTML programmers maintain your JSPs, which is very common, then they are going to have to have a pretty good understanding of Java. This results in a very unclear definition of the programmer's role. It also calls for a very skilled programmer.

A Server-Side Implementation of the MVC

The real power of JSPs and servlets come into being when they are used together. In this section, we define a server-side implementation of the MVC, where the *Model* is a JavaBean, a shopping cart, that represents the data being transmitted or received. The *Controller* is a servlet that manipulates or transmits data, and the *View* is a JSP that presents the results of the performed transaction. Figure 16.1 models the steps involved in a server-side implementation of the MVC.

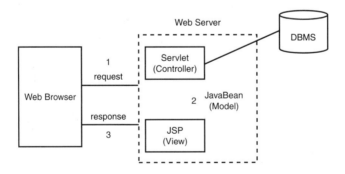

Figure 16.1

The steps in a server-side MVC.

These steps are as follows:

1. The Web browser makes a request to the Controller servlet.
2. The servlet performs necessary manipulations to the `JavaBean` Model and forwards the result to the JSP View.
3. The JSP formats the Model for display and sends the HTML results back to the Web browser.

A Server-Side Example Using the MVC

In this section, we create an MVC implementation using the Shopping Cart example we used in Chapter 13, "JSP and a Shopping Cart."

We will be using the following files from Chapter 13:

- `ShoppingCart.java`
- `AddToShoppingCart.jsp`
- `ShoppingCart.jsp`

The first thing we are going to do is to remove scriptlet code used to add an item to the `ShoppingCart` from the `AddToShoppingCart.jsp` we used in Chapter 13. We will also need to change the `action` attribute of the form we used to point to our controller servlet instead of the JSP. You should notice how little scriptlet code is contained in our new JSP. Listing 16.1 contains the source for our changes. The new file is called `AddToShoppingCartMVC.jsp`.

Listing 16.1   AddToShoppingCartMVC.jsp

```
<%@ page errorPage="errorpage.jsp" %>

<!-- Instantiate the ShoppingCart bean with an id of "cart" -->
<jsp:useBean id="cart" scope="session" class="ShoppingCart" />

<html>
  <head>
    <title>DVD Catalog</title>
  </head>
  <body>
  <!-- Print the current quantity of the ShoppingCart -->
  <a href="/purejsp/ShoppingCartMVC.jsp">Shopping Cart Quantity:</a>
    <%=cart.getNumOfItems() %>
  <hr>
  <center><h3>DVD Catalog</h3></center>
  <table border="1" width="300" cellspacing="0"
  cellpadding="2" align="center">
    <tr><th>Description</th><th>Price</th></tr>
<!-- ("123", "First thing added", 123.45f, 4); -->
    <tr>
      <form action="/purejsp/servlet/ShopController" method" "post">
        <td>Happy Gilmore</td>
        <td>$19.95</td>
```

continues

Listing 16.1   continued

```
      <td><input type="submit" name="Submit" value="Add"></td>
      <input type="hidden" name="id" value="1">
      <input type="hidden" name="desc" value="Happy Gilmore">
      <input type="hidden" name="price" value="19.95">
      <input type="hidden" name="command" value="add">
    </form>
  </tr>
  <tr>
    <form action="/purejsp/servlet/ShopController" method="post">
    <td>Wayne's World</td>
    <td>$19.95</td>
    <td><input type="submit" name="Submit" value="Add"></td>
    <input type="hidden" name="id" value="2">
    <input type="hidden" name="desc" value="Wayne's World">
    <input type="hidden" name="price" value="19.95">
    <input type="hidden" name="command" value="add">
    </form>
  </tr>
  <tr>
    <form action="/purejsp/servlet/ShopController" method="post">
    <td>Tommy Boy</td>
    <td>$15.95</td>
    <td><input type="submit" name="Submit" value="Add"></td>
    <input type="hidden" name="id" value="3">
    <input type="hidden" name="desc" value="Tommy Boy">
    <input type="hidden" name="price" value="15.95">
    <input type="hidden" name="command" value="add">
    </form>
  </tr>
  <tr>
    <form action="/purejsp/servlet/ShopController" method="post">
    <td>Lethal Weapon 4</td>
    <td>$19.95</td>
    <td><input type="submit" name="Submit" value="Add"></td>
    <input type="hidden" name="id" value="4">
    <input type="hidden" name="desc" value="Lethal Weapon 4">
    <input type="hidden" name="price" value="19.95">
    <input type="hidden" name="command" value="add">
    </form>
  </tr>
  <tr>
    <form action="/purejsp/servlet/ShopController" method="post">
    <td>Nutty Professor</td>
    <td>$19.95</td>
    <td><input type="submit" name="Submit" value="Add"></td>
    <input type="hidden" name="id" value="5">
    <input type="hidden" name="desc" value="Nutty Professor">
    <input type="hidden" name="price" value="19.95">
```

```
      <input type="hidden" name="command" value="add">
    </form>
  </tr>
  </table>
 </body>
</html>
```

Our next step includes creating a servlet that will act as a controller for all shopping cart–related transactions. Listing 16.2 contains the source for our controller servlet.

Listing 16.2   ShopController.java

```java
import javax.servlet.*;
import javax.servlet.http.*;
import java.io.*;
import java.util.*;

import ShoppingCart;

public class ShopController extends HttpServlet {

  //Initialize global variables
  public void init(ServletConfig config)
    throws ServletException {

    super.init(config);
  }

  //Process the HTTP Post request
  public void doPost(HttpServletRequest request,
    HttpServletResponse response)
    throws ServletException, IOException {

    String command = request.getParameter("command");
    HttpSession session = request.getSession();
    ShoppingCart cart = (ShoppingCart)session.getAttribute("cart");

    // Determine which command to perform
    if ( command.equals("add") ) {

      // Get the item from the request
      String id = request.getParameter("id");
      if ( id != null ) {

        String desc = request.getParameter("desc");
        Float price = new Float(request.getParameter("price"));

        // Add the selected item to the cart
        cart.addItem(id, desc, price.floatValue(), 1);
      }
```

continues

Listing 16.2   continued

```
      }
      // Redirect the response
      // after adding an item to the cart.
      response.sendRedirect("/purejsp/AddToShoppingCartMVC.jsp");
  }

  //Get Servlet information
  public String getServletInfo() {

    return "ShopController Information";
  }
}
```

As you look over this servlet, you will notice that it simply checks the request for the command it should perform. In our case we only use one command add, which gets the item's attributes from the request and adds a new item to the shopping cart. It then forwards the response back to the calling JSP for display. One thing you should notice is that the ShopController servlet contains no presentation code. It simply performs the necessary transaction and then leaves it up to the JSP to handle presentation.

Separating the presentation from the content in this manner makes it possible to change the presentation layer without making any changes to the servlet code. This is where the real power exists in using JSPs and servlets.

The final step we need to perform is changing the *Back to Catalog* link that is found in our ShoppingCart.jsp to point to our new AddToShoppingCartMVC.jsp. The new file is ShoppingCartMVC.jsp, and the source can be found in Listing 16.3.

Listing 16.3   ShoppingCartMVC.jsp

```
<%@ page errorPage="errorpage.jsp" %>
<%@ page import="java.util.*" %>

<!-- Instantiate the ShoppingCart bean with an id of "cart" -->
<jsp:useBean id="cart" scope="session" class="ShoppingCart" />

<html>
  <head>
    <title>Shopping Cart Contents</title>
  </head>
  <body>
    <center>
    <table width="300" border="1" cellspacing="0"
      cellpadding="2" border="0">
      <caption><b>Shopping Cart Contents</b></caption>
      <tr>
```

```
        <th>Description</th>
        <th>Price</th>
        <th>Quantity</th>
      </tr>
    <%
      Enumeration enum = cart.getEnumeration();
      String[] tmpItem;
      // Iterate over the cart
      while (enum.hasMoreElements()) {

        tmpItem = (String[])enum.nextElement();
      %>
        <tr>
          <td><%=tmpItem[1] %></td>
          <td align="center">$<%=tmpItem[2] %></td>
          <td align="center"><%=tmpItem[3] %></td>
        </tr>
        <%
      }
    %>
    </table>
    </center>
    <a href="/purejsp/AddToShoppingCartMVC.jsp">Back to Catalog</a>
  </body>
</html>
```

That is all there is to it. To make it a really functional application, you should probably add some more transactions, but this only involves adding new commands. To see our new MVC application in action, you should make sure the ShoppingCart.java and the ShopController.java files are compiled and moved to the <SERVER_ROOT>/purejsp/WEB-INF/classes/ directory. You should also move the AddToShoppingCartMVC.jsp and ShoppingCartMVC.jsp files to the <SERVER_ROOT>/purejsp/ directory. Now open your browser to the following URL:

```
http://localhost:8080/purejsp/AddToShoppingCartMVC.jsp
```

You will see a page similar to Figure 16.2.

After you have loaded the initial JSP, go ahead and add items to the cart and view the contents of the cart by selecting the Shopping Cart Quantity link. You will see a page similar to Figure 16.3.

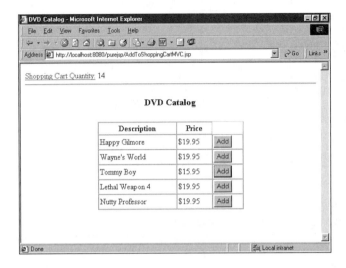

Figure 16.2

Output from AddToShoppingCartMVC.jsp.

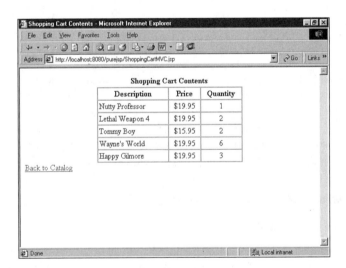

Figure 16.3

Output from ShoppingCartMVC.jsp.

Summary

In this chapter, we talked about the Model-View-Controller design pattern. We discussed the drawbacks of a servlet- or JSP-only application model. And finally we looked at how we could solve the problems encountered by the JSPs and servlets-only application model, by leveraging the MVC design pattern.

In Chapter 17, we cover how to work with JavaMail and JSPs.

CHAPTER 17

JSP and JavaMail

Traditionally when you needed to interact with a mail server from within code, you encountered a messy collection of socket code containing a lot of string parsing. The code would have to send a request to the server, wait for the response, and then break down the response to parse the necessary information. The JavaMail API has provided a clean and easy-to-use Java interface to design and implement messaging and Internet email solutions.

Internet email is comprised of several standards detailing the format and makeup of a message that is to be sent across the Internet. There are also standards, as well as some proposed standards, that dictate how Internet email services handle the messages.

The two types of services that JavaMail offers are the transport and store services. The transport service has several jobs, but we will simply think of it as the service that takes our message and sends it to the recipient. The message may make several stops along the way, but the intricacies of these stops are not within the scope of this book.

The second type of service that a JavaMail system deals with is the store service. The store manipulates the persistent storage of messages. The storage of messages is done in what most of us know as *mailboxes*, for example, your inbox. JavaMail refers to these mailboxes as *folders* because it is possible for one folder to contain other folders, messages, or both. The physical structure of the folders on a mail server depends on the mail server used to create and manage them. So, to put it simply, a store service allows you to read and manipulate your folders and messages.

Store and *transport* are generic terms used by the JavaMail API to refer to the protocols that actually implement these services. In the case of Internet email, the most widely used transport protocol is the Simple Mail Transfer Protocol (SMTP). The most widely used protocols that implement the store service are the Post Office Protocol (POP3) and Internet Message Access Protocol (IMAP4).

JavaMail gives you an interface to a messaging system. In order for it to be useful, you also require service providers that implement the JavaMail API. Packaged with the JavaMail API, Sun Microsystems has supplied you with both an SMTP and an IMAP service provider. A POP provider can be downloaded through Sun. These providers are their implementation of the JavaMail API, designed to interact with each of the different protocols. Anyone can write his own implementation, to interact with these or other protocols. The document "The JavaMail Guide for Service Providers" is packaged with the JavaMail archive and specifies how to develop and package a service provider.

Configuring JavaMail

Before we get started, you probably want to know what you will need in order to use the JavaMail API, and where to get it. The JavaMail API can be downloaded from

`http://www.javasoft.com/products/javamail/index.html`

The archive you will get contains the JavaMail API jar file, all of the javadoc files, the JavaMail Specification in PDF format, the guide for service providers in PDF format, and a decent collection of demo code with documentation.

JavaMail makes extensive use of the JavaBeans Activation Framework (JAF). So, you will also need to download this Java extension. It can be found at

`http://www.javasoft.com/beans/glasgow/jaf.html`

This archive contains a collection of files similar to the JavaMail archive. The two important files you will need are the `mail.jar` and `activation.jar` files. Both of these archives must be added to your classpath before you can begin working with JavaMail.

A JavaMail Example

Let's walk through a simple example of sending a message using JavaMail.

NOTE

The JavaMail API provides an interface to perform many more complex tasks, including sending MIME-encoded attachments to your mail. And, as we discussed earlier, you can retrieve and manipulate messages from your mailboxes. The demo code that accompanies JavaMail gives good examples of some of the other features that you can use. With a little creativity, you are not limited to what you can accomplish.

Listing 17.1 contains our JavaMail example.

Listing 17.1   SimpleSendMessage.java

```java
import java.util.*;

import javax.mail.*;
import javax.mail.internet.*;
import javax.activation.*;

public class SimpleSendMessage {

  public static void main(String[] args) {

    // Collect the necessary information to send a simple message
    // Make sure to replace the values for host, to, and from with
    // valid information.
    // host - must be a valid smtp server that you currently have
    //          access to.
    // to - whoever is going to get your email
    // from - whoever you want to be. Just remember that many smtp
    //          servers will validate the domain of the from address
    //          before allowing the mail to be sent.
    String host = "server.myhost.com";
    String to = "YourFriend@somewhere.com";
    String from = "MeMeMe@myhost.com";
    String subject = "JSP Rules!";
    String messageText = "I am sending a message using the"
      + " JavaMail API.\n"
  + "I can include any text that I want.";
    boolean sessionDebug = false;

    // Create some properties and get the default Session.
    Properties props = System.getProperties();
      props.put("mail.host", host);
      props.put("mail.transport.protocol", "smtp");

    Session session = Session.getDefaultInstance(props, null);

    // Set debug on the Session so we can see what is going on
    // Passing false will not echo debug info, and passing true
    // will.
      session.setDebug(sessionDebug);

    try {

      // Instantiate a new MimeMessage and fill it with the
      // required information.
      Message msg = new MimeMessage(session);
```

continues

Listing 17.1   continued

```
      msg.setFrom(new InternetAddress(from));
      InternetAddress[] address = {new InternetAddress(to)};
      msg.setRecipients(Message.RecipientType.TO, address);
      msg.setSubject(subject);
      msg.setSentDate(new Date());
      msg.setText(messageText);

      // Hand the message to the default transport service
      // for delivery.
      Transport.send(msg);
    }
    catch (MessagingException mex) {

      mex.printStackTrace();
    }
  }
}
```

In analyzing Listing 17.1, the first topic we must discuss is the `Session` class. The `Session` represents a mail session and is typically the first thing that you will set up in code using the JavaMail API. It collects properties and defaults that will be used by different pieces throughout the API.

In the following code snippet, we retrieve the system properties, add the JavaMail–specific information to them, and retrieve a default `Session` using them. The properties we use here are just some of the JavaMail–specific attributes that can be used; however, they are the only ones necessary to accomplish sending a simple message:

```
String host = "server.myhost.com";
String to = "YourFriend@somewhere.com";
String from = "MeMeMe@myhost.com";
String subject = "JSP Rules!";
String messageText = "I am sending a message using the"
  + " JavaMail API.\nI can include any text that I want.";
  boolean sessionDebug = false;

// Create some properties and get the default Session.
Properties props = System.getProperties();
props.put("mail.host", host);
props.put("mail.transport.protocol", "smtp");

Session session = Session.getDefaultInstance(props, null);
```

The `mail.host` environment property specifies the default mail server. In many cases the server for transport and store are the same machine. However, they can be specified separately if this is not the case. For our purposes it does not matter, because we will only need access to the transport service.

NOTE

You will need to change the mail host in the application to use your ISP's mail host.

Using the `mail.transport.protocol` property tells the `Session` what protocol to use as the default transport provider. We specified `smtp` as the default transport, so the `Session` now knows that whenever we use a transport this is the service provider we want. This becomes important later when we actually send the message, because we use a static method in the `Transport` class to send and we never specify what type of transport we want to use.

In the next code snippet, we create a message and prepare it to be shipped off. There is quite a bit more that can take place before a message is sent, but we are only interested in the bare necessities:

```
String to = "YourFriend@somewhere.com";
String from = "MeMeMe@myhost.com";
String subject = "JSP Rules!";
String messageText =
   "I am sending a message using the JavaMail API.\n"
   + "I can include any text that I want.";

Message msg = new MimeMessage(session);

msg.setFrom(new InternetAddress(from));
InternetAddress[] address = {new InternetAddress(to)};
msg.setRecipients(Message.RecipientType.TO, address);
msg.setSubject(subject);
msg.setSentDate(new Date());
msg.setText(messageText);
```

The first thing you may notice is the use of the `MimeMessage` class. It implements the `Message` abstract class, and uses certain criteria to make sure the message adheres to the Internet email standards. It formats the message and message headers in the proper MIME style to be sent over the Internet. (A discussion on the MIME Standard is beyond the scope of this book.)

The next several method calls fill the message with the needed information. Addresses used by a `MimeMessage` are implemented by the `InternetAddress` class. You will notice that this class is used for both the sender and recipients. Neither the subject nor the content of the message are required to successfully transport the message, but, let's face it, how exciting would it be without them?

Now that the Message is prepared to be sent, all we have to do is ask our default transport provider to send it for us. The code snippet to accomplish this is simple and looks like this:

```
Transport.send(msg);
```

That is all there is to sending a simple email using the JavaMail API.

Using JavaMail in a JSP

Next we look at what is necessary to send an email using JavaMail and JSP. For our JSP example, we are going to use an HTML form to submit the mail message and a JSP to parse and send the submitted message. The HTML form can be found in Listing 17.2.

Listing 17.2   MailForm.html

```html
<html>
  <head>
    <title>JavaMail Form</title>
  </head>

<body>
  <form action="/purejsp/MailExample.jsp" method="post">
    <table cellspacing="2" cellpadding="2" border="1">
      <tr>
        <td>To:</td>
        <td>
          <input type="text" name="to" size="30" maxlength="30">
        </td>
      </tr>
      <tr>
        <td>From:</td>
        <td>
          <input type="text" name="from" size="30" maxlength="30">
        </td>
      </tr>
      <tr>
        <td>Subject</td>
        <td>
          <input type="text" name="subject" size="30" maxlength="30">
        </td>
      </tr>
      <tr>
        <td colspan="2">
          <textarea cols="40" rows="10" name="body"></textarea>
        </td>
      </tr>
      <tr>
        <td>
          <input type="submit" name="submit" value="Submit">
```

```
        <input type="Reset">
      </td>
    </tr>
  </table>
 </form>
</body>
</html>
```

You can see that there is nothing special about our form. You should only notice the action attribute of the `form` points to our JSP, found in Listing 17.3.

Listing 17.3   `MailExample.jsp`

```
<html>
  <head>
    <title>JSP JavaMail Example </title>
  </head>

<body>

<%@ page import="java.util.*" %>
<%@ page import="javax.mail.*" %>
<%@ page import="javax.mail.internet.*" %>
<%@ page import="javax.activation.*" %>

<%
    String host = "yourmailhost";
    String to = request.getParameter("to");
    String from = request.getParameter("from");
    String subject = request.getParameter("subject");
    String messageText = request.getParameter("body");
    boolean sessionDebug = false;

    // Create some properties and get the default Session.
    Properties props = System.getProperties();
      props.put("mail.host", host);
      props.put("mail.transport.protocol", "smtp");

    Session mailSession = Session.getDefaultInstance(props, null);

    // Set debug on the Session so we can see what is going on
    // Passing false will not echo debug info, and passing true
    // will.
    mailSession.setDebug(sessionDebug);

    // Instantiate a new MimeMessage and fill it with the
    // required information.
    Message msg = new MimeMessage(mailSession);
```

continues

Listing 17.1   continued

```
    msg.setFrom(new InternetAddress(from));
    InternetAddress[] address = {new InternetAddress(to)};
    msg.setRecipients(Message.RecipientType.TO, address);
    msg.setSubject(subject);
    msg.setSentDate(new Date());
    msg.setText(messageText);

    // Hand the message to the default transport service
    // for delivery.
    Transport.send(msg);

    out.println("Mail was sent to " + to);
    out.println(" from " + from);
    out.println(" using host " + host + ".");

%>
    </table>
  </body>
</html>
```

As you look over the MailExample.jsp, you will notice only a few differences from our previously covered JavaMail application. The first change is just the addition of the code to get the necessary request parameters, which is included in the following snippet:

```
String to = request.getParameter("to");
String from = request.getParameter("from");
String subject = request.getParameter("subject");
String messageText = request.getParameter("body");
```

The only other notable change is that, instead of referring to the Session with the variable name session, we have changed the variable name to mailSession. It still holds a reference to the mail Session. It was changed because of the JSP implicit variable session, which references the HttpSession.

To see the MailExample.jsp in action, copy both the HTML file and the JSP file to the <SERVER_ROOT>/purejsp/ directory and load the following URL into your browser:

```
http://localhost:8080/purejsp/MailForm.html
```

You should see a page similar to Figure 17.1.

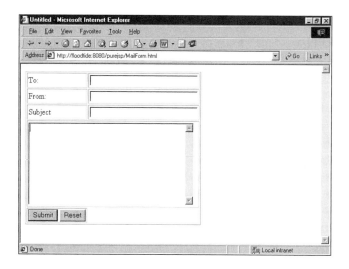

Figure 17.1

Output of the MailForm.html.

Now fill in the appropriate form data and click the Submit button. You should see a response that tells you who received the mail, who sent the mail, and the mail host. To test the example, it is probably best to send mail to yourself, so you can check the message.

Summary

In this chapter, we covered what JavaMail is and how you use it. We also took a look at how you can use JavaMail with JSPs.

This is the last techniques chapter in this book. Chapter 18, "The javax.servlet.jsp Package," begins the reference section of this text.

PART III

SYNTAX REFERENCE
(WITH UML DIAGRAMS)

CHAPTER 18

The javax.servlet.jsp Package

The `javax.servlet.jsp` package makes up the bulk of the JavaServer Pages API. It is covered completely in this chapter. Figure 18.1 contains the `javax.servlet.jsp` object model.

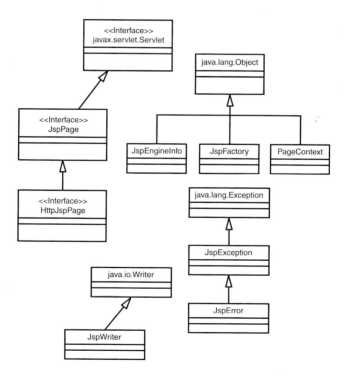

Figure 18.1

`javax.servlet.jsp` *object model.*

Interfaces

The javax.servlet.jsp package has two interfaces, HttpJspPage and JspPage.

HttpJspPage Interface

```
public interface HttpJspPage extends JspPage
```

This is the interface that a JSP processor-generated class for the HTTP protocol must satisfy. It extends JspPage and defines a single method.

_jspService() Method

```
public void _jspService(
        javax.servlet.http.HttpServletRequest request,
        javax.servlet.http.HttpServletResponse response)
    throws javax.servlet.ServletException,
    java.io.IOException
```

The _jspService method corresponds to the body of the JSP page. It is defined automatically by the JSP processor and should never be redefined by the JSP author. It returns no value.

Parameters

- HttpServletRequest
- HttpServletResponse

Exceptions Thrown

- javax.servlet.ServletException
- java.io.IOException

JspPage Interface

```
public interface JspPage extends javax.servlet.Servlet
```

This is the interface that a JSP processor-generated class must implement.

The interface defines a protocol with three methods; only two of them, jspInit() and jspDestroy(), are part of this interface. The signature of the third method, _jspService(), depends on the specific protocol used and cannot be expressed in a generic way in Java.

A class implementing this interface is responsible for invoking the first two methods at the appropriate time based on the corresponding servlet-based method invocations.

The jspInit() and jspDestroy() methods can be defined by a JSP author, but the _jspService() method is defined automatically by the JSP processor based on the contents of the JSP page.

jspInit() Method

```
public void jspInit()
```

The jspInit() method is invoked when the JspPage is initialized. Once the JSP page is initialized, the getServletConfig() method will return the desired value. It is synonymous with the init() method of a servlet. It has no parameters, returns no value, and throws no exceptions.

jspDestroy() Method

`public void jspDestroy()`

The jspDestroy () is invoked when the JSP page is about to be destroyed. It is synonymous with the destroy() method of a servlet. It has no parameters, returns no value, and throws no exceptions.

Classes

The javax.servlet.jsp package has four classes: JspEngineInfo, JspFactory, JspWriter, and PageContext.

JspEngineInfo Class

`public abstract class JspEngineInfo`

The JspEngineInfo class is an abstract class that provides information on the current JSP engine. The class has two methods, described in the following sections.

JspEngineInfo() Method

`public JspEngineInfo()`

The JspEngineInfo() method is an empty default constructor. It has no parameters, returns no value, and throws no exceptions.

getImplementationVersion() Method

`public java.lang.String getImplementationVersion()`

The getImplementationVersion() method returns the current version of the JSP specification. The version number must begin with a number. If the version is not defined, then a null will be returned. It has no parameters and throws no exceptions.

Returns

• java.lang.String

JspFactory Class

`public abstract class JspFactory extends java.lang.Object`

JspFactory is an abstract class that defines a number of factory methods available to a JSP page at runtime for the purposes of creating instances of various interfaces and classes used to support the JSP implementation. The JspFactory class has one field and six methods, as described in the following sections.

deflt Field

```
private static JspFactory deflt
```

The deflt field represents the default JspFactory implementation.

JspFactory() Method

```
public JspFactory()
```

The JspFactory() method is an empty default constructor. It has no parameters, returns no value, and throws no exceptions.

setDefaultFactory() Method

```
public static void setDefaultFactory(JspFactory deflt)
```

The setDefaultFactory() method sets the default factory for this JSP implementation. It is illegal for any principal other than the JSP runtime engine to call this method. It returns no value and throws no exceptions.

Parameters

• JspFactory

getDefaultFactory() Method

```
public static JspFactory getDefaultFactory()
```

The getDefaultFactory() method returns the default factory for this JSP implementation. It has no parameters and throws no exceptions.

Returns

• JspFactory

getPageContext() Method

```
public abstract PageContext getPageContext(
      javax.servlet.Servlet servlet,
      javax.servlet.ServletRequest request,
      javax.servlet.ServletResponse response,
      java.lang.String errorPageURL,
      boolean needsSession,
      int buffer,
      boolean autoflush)
```

The getPageContext() method obtains an instance of an implementation-dependent javax.servlet.jsp.PageContext abstract class for the calling servlet and currently pending request and response. This method is typically called early in the processing of the _jspService() method of a JSP implementation class in order to obtain a PageContext object for the request being processed. Invoking this method will result in the PageContext.initialize() method being invoked. The returned object is a properly initialized PageContext. All PageContext objects obtained via this method must be released by invoking releasePageContext(). getPageContext() throws no exceptions.

Parameters

- javax.servlet.Servlet
- javax.servlet.ServletRequest
- javax.servlet.ServletResponse
- java.lang.String
- boolean
- int
- boolean

Returns

- PageContext

releasePageContext() Method

public void releasePageContext(PageContext pc)

The releasePageContext() method is called to release a previously allocated PageContext object returned from a call to getPageContext(). This method should be invoked prior to returning from the _jspService() method of a JSP implementation class. releasePageContext() returns no value and throws no exceptions.

Parameters

- PageContext

getEngineInfo() Method

public JspEngineInfo getEngineInfo()

The getEngineInfo() method is called to get implementation-specific information on the current JSP engine. It has no parameters and throws no exceptions.

Returns

- JspEngineInfo

JspWriter Class

public abstract class JspWriter extends java.io.Writer

JspWriter is an abstract class that emulates some of the functionality found in the java.io.BufferedWriter and java.io.PrintWriter classes. However, JspWriter differs from these other classes in that it throws a java.io.IOException from the print methods where PrintWriter does not. JspWriter class has four fields and numerous methods, as described in the following sections.

NO_BUFFER Field

`public static final int NO_BUFFER`

This field is a constant indicating that the writer is not buffering output.

DEFAULT_BUFFER Field

`public static final int DEFAULT_BUFFER`

This field is a constant indicating that the writer is buffered and is using the implementation default buffer size.

bufferSize Field

`protected int bufferSize`

This field indicates the writer's buffer size.

autoFlush Field

`protected boolean autoFlush`

This field indicates whether the buffer will be automatically flushed.

JspWriter() Method

`protected JspWriter(int bufferSize, boolean autoFlush)`

The `JspWriter()` method is a protected constructor. It returns no value and throws no exceptions.

Parameters

- `int`
- `boolean`

newLine() Method

`public void newLine() throws java.io.IOException`

Exceptions Thrown

- `java.io.IOException`

print(boolean b) Method

`public void print(boolean b) throws java.io.IOException`

This `print(boolean b)` method prints a Boolean value. The string produced by `String.valueOf(boolean)` is translated into bytes according to the platform's default character encoding.

NOTE

The print() method prints data type values, which are translated into bytes. For all values, these bytes are written in exactly the same manner as the Writer.write(int) method.

NOTE

The print() method's parameter is determined by the print value. The method always throws a java.io.IOException exception. For all print values, the print() method returns no value.

Parameters

- boolean

print(char c) Method

public void print(char c) throws java.io.IOException

This print() method prints a character value. The character is translated into one or more bytes according to the platform's default character encoding.

Parameters

- char

print(int i) Method

public void print(int i) throws java.io.IOException

This print(int i) method prints an integer. The string produced by String.valueOf(int) is translated into bytes according to the platform's default character encoding.

Parameters

- int

print(long l) Method

public void print(long l) throws java.io.IOException

This print(long l) method prints a long. The string produced by String.valueOf(long) is translated into bytes according to the platform's default character encoding.

Parameters

- long

print(float f) Method

public void print(float f) throws java.io.IOException

This `print(float f)` method prints a float. The string produced by `String.valueOf(float)` is translated into bytes according to the platform's default character encoding.

Parameters

- `float`

print(double d) Method

```
public void print(double d) throws java.io.IOException
```

This `print(double d)` method prints a double. The string produced by `String.valueOf(double)` is translated into bytes according to the platform's default character encoding.

Parameters

- `double`

print(char[] s) Method

```
public void print(char[] s) throws java.io.IOException
```

This `print(char[] s)` method prints an array of characters. The characters are converted into bytes according to the platform's default character encoding.

Parameters

- `char[]`

print(java.lang.String s) Method

```
public void print(java.lang.String s) throws java.io.IOException
```

The `print(java.lang.String s)` method prints a string. If the argument is null, then the string `null` is printed. Otherwise, the string's characters are converted into bytes according to the platform's default character encoding.

Parameters

- `java.lang.String`

print(java.lang.Object obj) Method

```
public void print(java.lang.Object obj) throws java.io.IOException
```

This `print()` method prints an object. The string produced by the `String.valueOf(Object)` method is translated into bytes according to the platform's default character encoding.

Parameters

- `java.lang.Object`

println() Method

`public void println() throws java.io.IOException`

This `println()` method terminates the current line by writing the line separator string. The line separator string is defined by the system property `line.separator`, and is not necessarily a single newline character (\n). This method has no parameters.

> **NOTE**
>
> The `println()` method always throws a `java.io.IOException` exception. It returns no value.

println(boolean b) Method

`public void println(boolean b) throws java.io.IOException`

This `println(boolean b)` method prints a Boolean value and then terminates the line. This method behaves as though it invokes `print(boolean)` and then `println()`.

Parameters

- `boolean`

println(char c) Method

`public void println(char c) throws java.io.IOException`

This `println(char c)` method prints a character and then terminates the line. This method behaves as though it invokes `print(char)` and then `println()`.

Parameters

- `char`

println(int i) Method

`public void println(int i) throws java.io.IOException`

This `println(int i)` method prints an integer and then terminates the line. This method behaves as though it invokes `print(int)` and then `println()`.

Parameters

- `int`

println(long l) Method

`public void println(long l) throws java.io.IOException`

This `println(long l)` method prints a long integer and then terminates the line. This method behaves as though it invokes `print(long)` and then `println()`.

Parameters

- `long`

println(float f) Method

```
public void println(float f) throws java.io.IOException
```

This `println(float f)` method prints a float and then terminates the line. This method behaves as though it invokes `print(float)` and then `println()`.

Parameters

- float

println(double d) Method

```
public void println(double d) throws java.io.IOException
```

This `println(double d)` method prints a double-precision floating-point number and then terminates the line. This method behaves as though it invokes `print(double)` and then `println()`.

Parameters

- double

println(char[] s) Method

```
public void println(char[] s) throws java.io.IOException
```

This `println(char[] s)` method prints an array of characters and then terminates the line. This method behaves as though it invokes `print(char[])` and then `println()`.

Parameters

- char[]

println(java.lang.String s) Method

```
public void println(java.lang.String s) throws java.io.IOException
```

The `println(java.lang.String s)` method prints a String and then terminates the line. This method behaves as though it invokes `print(String)` and then `println()`.

Parameters

- java.lang.String

println(java.lang.Object obj) Method

```
public void println(java.lang.Object obj) throws java.io.IOException
```

This `println()` method prints an object and then terminates the line. This method behaves as though it invokes `print(Object)` and then `println()`.

Parameters

- java.lang.Object

clear() Method

```
public void clear() throws java.io.IOException
```

The clear() method clears the contents of the buffer. If the buffer has already been flushed, then the clear operation throws an IOException to signal the fact that some data has already been irrevocably written to the client response stream. The method has no parameters.

clearBuffer() Method

```
public void clearBuffer() throws java.io.IOException
```

The clearBuffer() method clears the current contents of the buffer. Unlike clear(), this method will not throw an IOException if the buffer has already been flushed. It merely clears the current content of the buffer and returns. clearBuffer() has no parameters.

flush() Method

```
public void flush() throws java.io.IOException
```

The flush() method flushes the stream. If the stream has saved any characters from the various write() methods in a buffer, flush() writes them immediately to their intended destination. Then, if that destination is another character or byte stream, the method flushes it. Thus, one flush() invocation will flush all the buffers in a chain of writers and output streams. flush() has no parameters.

close() Method

```
public void close() throws java.io.IOException
```

The close() method closes the stream, flushing it first. Once a stream has been closed, further write() or flush() invocations will cause an IOException to be thrown. Closing a previously closed stream, however, has no effect. close() has no parameters.

getBufferSize() Method

```
public int getBufferSize() throws java.io.IOException
```

The getBufferSize() method returns the size of the buffer in bytes, or 0, if there is no buffer. It has no parameters.

Returns

- int

Exceptions Thrown

- java.io.IOException

getRemaining() Method

```
public int getRemaining() throws java.io.IOException
```

The getRemaining() method returns the number of bytes unused in the buffer. It has no parameters.

Returns

- int

Exceptions Thrown

- java.io.IOException

isAutoFlush() Method

```
public boolean isAutoFlush()
```

The isAutoFlush() method returns whether auto-flush is on or not. It has no parameters.

Returns

- boolean

Exceptions Thrown

- java.io.IOException

PageContext Class

```
public abstract class PageContext extends java.lang.Object
```

The PageContext class is an abstract class, designed to be extended, to provide implementation-dependent implementations, by the JSP runtime environments. A PageContext instance is obtained by a JSP implementation class by calling the JspFactory.getPageContext() method; it is released by calling JspFactory.releasePageContext().

The PageContext object provides a number of useful tools to the page or component author and the page implementer. A list of some of these tools includes

- A single API to manage the various scoped namespaces
- A number of convenience APIs to access various public objects
- A mechanism to obtain the JspWriter for output
- A mechanism to manage session usage by the page
- A mechanism to expose page directive attributes to the scripting environment
- Mechanisms to forward or include the current request to other active components in the application
- A mechanism to handle errorpage exception processing

The PageContext class has numerous fields and methods, as described in the following sections.

APPLICATION Field

`public static final java.lang.String APPLICATION`

The `APPLICATION` field indicates a name used to store `ServletContext` in the `PageContext` name table.

APPLICATION_SCOPE Field

`public static final int APPLICATION_SCOPE`

This field indicates that a named reference remains available in the `ServletContext` until it is reclaimed.

CONFIG Field

`public static final java.lang.String CONFIG`

This field indicates a name used to store `ServletConfig` in the `PageContext` name table.

EXCEPTION Field

`public static final java.lang.String EXCEPTION`

This field indicates a name used to store an uncaught exception in the `ServletRequest` attribute list and the `PageContext` name table.

OUT Field

`public static final java.lang.String OUT`

This field indicates a name used to store the current `JspWriter` in the `PageContext` name table.

PAGE Field

`public static final java.lang.String PAGE`

This field indicates a name used to store the servlet in this `PageContext` name table.

PAGE_SCOPE Field

`public static final int PAGE_SCOPE`

This field indicates that the named reference remains available in this `PageContext` until its return from the current `Servlet.service()` invocation.

PAGECONTEXT Field

`public static final java.lang.String PAGECONTEXT`

This field indicates a name used to store this `PageContext` in its own name tables.

REQUEST Field

```
public static final java.lang.String REQUEST
```

This field indicates a name used to store `ServletRequest` in the `PageContext` name table.

REQUEST_SCOPE Field

```
public static final int REQUEST_SCOPE
```

This field indicates that the named reference remains available from the `ServletRequest` associated with the servlet until the current request is completed.

RESPONSE Field

```
public static final java.lang.String RESPONSE
```

A name used to store `ServletResponse` in the `PageContext` name table.

SESSION Field

```
public static final java.lang.String SESSION
```

This field indicates a name used to store `HttpSession` in the `PageContext` name table.

SESSION_SCOPE Field

```
public static final int SESSION_SCOPE
```

This field indicates the named reference that determines the scope of the `HttpSession` (if any) associated with the servlet until the `HttpSession` is invalidated.

PageContext() Method

```
public PageContext()
```

The `PageContext()` method is an empty default constructor. It has no parameters, returns no value, and throws no exceptions.

findAttribute() Method

```
public abstract java.lang.Object findAttribute(java.lang.String name)
```

The `findAttribute()` method searches for the named attribute in page, request, session, and application scopes (in that respective order) and returns the value associated or `null`. `findAttribute()` throws no exceptions

Parameters

- `java.lang.String`

Returns

- `java.lang.Object`

forward() Method

```
public abstract void forward(java.lang.String relativeUrlPath)
        throws javax.servlet.ServletException,
        java.io.IOException
```

The forward() method is used to redirect, or "forward" the current ServletRequest and ServletResponse to another active component in the application.

If the relativeUrlPath begins with a "/", then the URL specified is calculated relative to the DOCROOT of the ServletContext for this JSP. If the path does not begin with a "/", then the URL specified is calculated relative to the URL of the request that was mapped to the calling JSP. forward() returns no value.

Parameters

- java.lang.String

Exceptions Thrown

- javax.servlet.ServletException
- java.io.IOException

getAttribute(java.lang.String name) Method

```
public abstract java.lang.Object getAttribute(java.lang.String name)
        throws NullPointerException,
        java.lang.IllegalArgumentException
```

The getAttribute() method returns the object associated with the name in the page scope or null.

Parameters

- java.lang.String

Returns

- java.lang.Object

Exceptions Thrown

- NullPointerException
- java.lang.IllegalArgumentException

getAttribute(java.lang.String name, int scope) Method

```
public abstract java.lang.Object getAttribute(java.lang.String name,
  int scope)
  throws NullPointerException,
  java.lang.IllegalArgumentException
```

The getAttribute() method returns the object associated with the name in the specified scope or null.

Parameters

- java.lang.String
- int

Returns

- java.lang.Object

Exceptions Thrown

- NullPointerException
- java.lang.IllegalArgumentException

getAttributeNamesInScope() Method

```
public abstract java.util.Enumeration getAttributeNamesInScope(int scope)
```

The getAttributeNamesInScope() method returns an enumeration of names of all the attributes in the specified scope. It throws no exceptions.

Parameters

- int

Returns

- java.util.Enumeration

getAttributesScope() Method

```
public abstract int getAttributesScope(java.lang.String name)
```

The getAttributesScope() method returns the scope of the object associated with the name specified or 0. It has no exceptions thrown.

Parameters

- java.lang.String

Returns

- int

getException() Method

```
public abstract java.lang.Exception getException()
```

The getException() method returns any exception passed to this as an errorpage. It has no parameters and throws no exceptions.

Returns

- java.lang.Exception

getOut() Method

```
public abstract javax.servlet.jsp.JspWriter getOut()
```

The getOut() method returns the current JspWriter stream being used for client response. It has no parameters and throws no exceptions.

Returns

- javax.servlet.jsp.JspWriter

getPage() Method

```
public abstract java.lang.Object getPage()
```

The getPage() method returns the Page implementation class instance associated with this PageContext. It has no parameters and throws no exceptions.

Returns

- java.lang.Object

getRequest() Method

```
public abstract javax.servlet.ServletRequest getRequest()
```

The getRequest() method returns the ServletRequest for this PageContext. It has no parameters and throws no exceptions.

Returns

- javax.servlet.ServletRequest

getResponse() Method

```
public abstract javax.servlet.ServletResponse getResponse()
```

The getResponse() method returns the ServletResponse for this PageContext. It has no parameters and throws no exceptions.

Returns

- javax.servlet.ServletResponse

getServletConfig() Method

```
public abstract javax.servlet.ServletConfig getServletConfig()
```

The getServletConfig() method returns the ServletConfig for this PageContext. It has no parameters and throws no exceptions.

Returns

- javax.servlet.ServletConfig

getServletContext() Method

```
public abstract javax.servlet.ServletContext getServletContext()
```

The getServletContext() method returns the ServletContext for this PageContext. It has no parameters and throws no exceptions.

Returns

- javax.servlet.ServletContext

getSession() Method

```
public abstract javax.servlet.http.HttpSession getSession()
```

The getSession() method returns the HttpSession for this PageContext or null. It has no parameters and throws no exceptions.

Returns

- javax.servlet.http.HttpSession

handlePageException() Method

```
public abstract void handlePageException(java.lang.Exception e)
        throws javax.servlet.ServletException,
        java.io.IOException
```

The handlePageException() method is intended to process an unhandled "page" level exception either by redirecting the exception to the specified error page for this JSP, or—if no error page was specified—by performing some implementation-dependent action. handlePageException() returns no value.

Parameters

- java.lang.Exception

Exceptions Thrown

- javax.servlet.ServletException
- java.io.IOException

include() Method

```
public abstract void include(java.lang.String relativeUrlPath)
        throws javax.servlet.ServletException,
        java.lang.IllegalArgumentException,
        java.lang.SecurityException,
        java.io.IOException
```

The include() method causes the resource specified to be processed as part of the current ServletRequest and ServletResponse being processed by the calling thread. The output of the target resource's processing of the request is written directly to the ServletResponse output stream.

The current JspWriter "out" for this JSP is flushed as a side effect of this call, prior to processing the include.

It is valid to call this method only from a thread executing within a _jspService()
method of a JSP. include() returns no value.

Parameters

- java.lang.String

Exceptions Thrown

- javax.servlet.ServletException
- java.io.IOException
- java.lang.IllegalArgumentException
- java.lang.SecurityException

initialize() Method

```
public abstract void initialize(javax.servlet.Servlet servlet,
        javax.servlet.ServletRequest request,
        javax.servlet.ServletResponse response,
        java.lang.String errorPageURL,
        boolean needsSession,
        int bufferSize,
        boolean autoFlush)
        throws java.io.IOException,
        java.lang.IllegalStateException,
        java.lang.IllegalArgumentException
```

The initialize() method is called to initialize an uninitialized PageContext so that
it may be used by a JSP Implementation class to service an incoming request and
response within its _jspService() method.

This method is typically called from JspFactory.getPageContext() in order to initialize state.

This method is required to create an initial JspWriter. Associate the "out" name in
page scope with this newly created object. initialize() returns no value.

Parameters

- javax.servlet.Servlet
- javax.servlet.ServletRequest
- javax.servlet.ServletResponse
- java.lang.String
- boolean
- int
- boolean

Exceptions Thrown

- java.io.IOException
- java.lang.IllegalStateException
- java.lang.IllegalArgumentException

popBody() Method

`public abstract JspWriter popBody()`

The `popBody()` method returns the previous `JspWriter` "out" saved by the matching `pushBody()`, and updates the value of the "out" attribute in the page scope attribute namespace of the `PageContext`. `popBody()` has no parameters and throws no exceptions.

- `JspWriter`

pushBody() Method

`public abstract BodyJspWriter pushBody()`

The `pushBody()` method returns a new `BodyJspWriter` object, saves the current "out" `JspWriter`, and updates the value of the "out" attribute in the page scope attribute namespace of the `PageContext`. `pushBody()` has no parameters and throws no exceptions.

Returns

- `BodyJspWriter`

Exceptions Thrown

- None

release() Method

`public abstract void release()`

The `release()` method "resets" the internal state of a `PageContext`, releasing all internal references, and preparing the `PageContext` for potential reuse by a later invocation of `initialize()`. This method is typically called from `JspFactory`. `releasePageContext()`. `release()` has no parameters, returns no value, and throws no exceptions.

removeAttribute(java.lang.String name) Method

`public abstract void removeAttribute(java.lang.String name)`

The `removeAttribute(java.lang.String name)` method removes the object reference associated with the specified name. It returns no value and throws no exceptions.

Parameters

- `java.lang.String`

removeAttribute(java.lang.String name, int scope) Method

`public abstract void removeAttribute(java.lang.String name,`
`        int scope)`

The removeAttribute() method removes the object reference associated with the specified name and scope. It returns no value and throws no exceptions.

Parameters

- java.lang.String
- int

setAttribute() Method

```
public abstract void setAttribute(java.lang.String name,
        java.lang.Object attribute)
        throws NullPointerException
```

The setAttribute() method registers the name and object specified with page scope semantics. It returns no value.

Parameters

- java.lang.String
- java.lang.Object

Exceptions Thrown

- NullPointerException

setAttribute(java.lang.String name, java.lang.Object o, int scope) Method

```
public abstract void setAttribute(java.lang.String name,
        java.lang.Object o,
        int scope)
        throws NullPointerException,
        java.lang.IllegalArgumentException
```

The setAttribute() method registers the name and object specified with appropriate scope semantics. It returns no value.

Parameters

- java.lang.String
- java.lang.Object
- int

Exceptions Thrown

- NullPointerException
- java.lang.IllegalArgumentException

Exceptions

The javax.servlet.jsp package has two exceptions, JspError and JspException. Each has two methods.

JspError Exception

```
public class JspError extends JspException
```

When the JspError exception is caught, output generation should stop and forward the exception to errorpage.

JspError(java.lang.String msg) Method

```
public JspError(java.lang.String msg)
```

The JspError(java.lang.String msg) method is a constructor with a message. It returns no value and throws no exceptions.

Parameters

• java.lang.String

JspError() Method

```
public JspError()
```

This method is a default empty constructor. It has no parameters, returns no value, and throws no exceptions.

JspException Exception

```
public class JspException extends java.lang.Exception
```

The JspException exception is a generic exception used by the JSP engine.

JspException(java.lang.String msg) Method

```
public JspException (java.lang.String msg)
```

This method is a constructor with a message. It returns no value and throws no exceptions.

Parameters

• java.lang.String

JspException() Method

```
public JspException ()
```

This method is a default empty constructor. It has no parameters, returns no value, and throws no exceptions.

Parameters

• None

Returns

• None

Exceptions Thrown

• None

CHAPTER 19

The javax.servlet. jsp.tagext Package

The JavaServer Pages 1.1 specification provides a portable mechanism for the description of tag libraries. Figure 19.1 contains the javax.servlet.jsp.tagext object model.

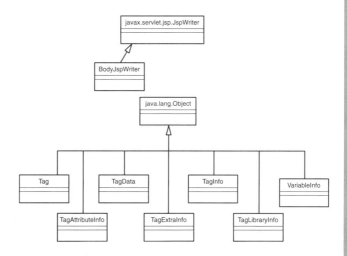

Figure 19.1

The javax.servlet.jsp.tagext *object model.*

Classes

The eight classes for the definition of JavaServer Pages tag libraries are described in the following sections. They are BodyJspWriter, Tag, TagAttributeInfo, TagData, TagExtraInfo, TagInfo, TagLibraryInfo, and VariableInfo.

BodyJspWriter Class

public abstract class BodyJspWriter extends JspWriter

BodyJspWriter is a JspWriter subclass that can be used to process body evaluations so they can be re-extracted at a later time. It has five methods.

BodyJspWriter() Method

protected BodyJspWriter(int buffersize, boolean autoflush)

This method is used to construct a BodyJspWriter. It should only to be used by a subclass. BodyJspWriter() returns no values and throws no exceptions.

Parameters

- int
- boolean

clearBody() Method

public void clearBody()

The clearBody() method is another implementation of the JspWriter method clear(). The only difference is that clearBody() is guaranteed not to throw an exception. clearBody() has no parameters and returns no value.

getReader() Method

public abstract java.io.Reader getReader()

The getReader() method returns the value of this BodyJspWriter as a Reader, after the BodyJspWriter has been processed. getReader() has no parameters and throws no exceptions.

Returns

- java.io.Reader

getString() Method

public abstract java.lang.String getString()

The getString() method returns the value of this BodyJspWriter as a String after the BodyJspWriter has been processed. It has no parameters and throws no exceptions.

Returns

- java.lang.String

writeOut() Method

public abstract void writeOut(java.io.Writer out)

The writeOut() method writes the contents of this BodyJspWriter into a Writer. It returns no value and throws no exceptions.

Parameters

- `java.io.Writer`

Tag Class

`public abstract class Tag extends java.lang.Object`

Actions in a tag library are defined through subclasses of the abstract class `Tag`. The class has 13 fields and 19 methods, as described in the following sections.

bodyOut Field

`protected BodyJspWriter bodyOut`

This field is used to hold the reference to the `BodyJspWriter`.

EVAL_BODY Field

`public static final int EVAL_BODY`

This field is used to hold the reference to the return value for `doStartTag()` and `doAfterBody()`.

EVAL_PAGE Field

`public static final int EVAL_PAGE`

This field is used to hold the reference to the return value for `doEndTag()`.

libraryPrefix Field

`private java.lang.String libraryPrefix`

This field is used to hold the prefix for the tag library of this tag.

pageContext Field

`protected PageContext pageContext`

This field is used to hold the reference to the current `PageContext`.

parent Field

`private Tag parent`

This field is a reference to the parent tag kept by each `Tag` instance, which effectively provides a runtime execution stack.

previousOut Field

`private JspWriter previousOut`

This field is a reference to the `JspWriter` and is valid when the tag is reached.

SKIP_BODY Field

```
public static final int SKIP_BODY
```

This field indicates whether the body of the action should be evaluated.

SKIP_PAGE Field

```
public static final int SKIP_PAGE
```

This field indicates whether or not the action should continue to evaluate the rest of the page.

tagData Field

```
protected TagData tagData
```

This field contains the value information for a tag instance.

tagId Field

```
private java.lang.String tagId
```

This field contains the value information for a tag id.

tagName Field

```
private java.lang.String tagName
```

This field contains a reference to the Tag's short name.

values Field

```
private java.util.Hashtable values
```

This field contains a reference to a Hashtable containing the Tags and their associated values.

Tag() Method

```
public Tag(java.lang.String libraryPrefix, java.lang.String tagName)
```

In this default constructor, all subclasses must define a public constructor with the same signature, and to call the superclass's constructor. This constructor is called by the code generated by the JSP translator. Tag() returns no value and throws no exceptions.

Parameters

- java.lang.String
- java.lang.String

doAfterBody() Method

```
public int doAfterBody() throws JspError
```

This method is invoked after every body evaluation. doAfterBody() has no parameters.

Returns

- `int`

Exceptions Thrown

- `JspError`

doBeforeBody() Method

`public int doBeforeBody() throws JspError`

This method is invoked before every body evaluation. `doBeforeBody()` has no parameters.

Returns

- `int`

Exceptions Thrown

- `JspError`

doEndTag() Method

`public int doEndTag() throws JspException`

This method processes the end tag. This method will be called on all `Tag` objects. It returns an indication of whether the rest of the page should be evaluated or skipped. `doEndTag()` has no parameters.

Returns

- `int`

Exceptions Thrown

- `JspException`

doStartTag() Method

`public int doStartTag() throws JspException`

This method processes the start tag for this instance. The `doStartTag()` method assumes that `initialize()` has been invoked prior to its own execution. When this method is invoked, the body has not yet been invoked. `doStartTag()` has no parameters.

Returns

- int

Exceptions Thrown

- `JspException`

findAncestorWithClass() Method

`public static final Tag findAncestorWithClass(Tag from,`
`    java.lang.Class class)`

This method finds the instance of a given class type that is closest to a given instance. This method is used for coordination among cooperating tags. `findAncestorWithClass()` throws no exceptions.

Parameters

- `Tag`
- `java.lang.Class`

Returns

- `Tag`

getBodyOut() Method

`protected final BodyJspWriter getBodyOut()`

This method returns the value of the current "out" `JspWriter`. `getBodyOut()` has no parameters and throws no exceptions.

Returns

- `BodyJspWriter`

getLibraryPrefix() Method

`public java.lang.String getLibraryPrefix()`

This method returns the library prefix being used with this tag. `getLibraryPrefix()` has no parameters and throws no exceptions.

Returns

- `java.lang.String`

getPageContext() Method

`public PageContext getPageContext()`

This method returns the `PageContext` for this tag. `getPageContext()` has no parameters and throws no exceptions.

Returns

- `PageContext`

getParent() Method

`public Tag getParent()`

This method returns the parent extension tag instance or null. `getParent()` has no parameters and throws no exceptions.

Returns

- `Tag`

getPreviousOut() Method

```
protected final JspWriter getPreviousOut()
```

This method returns the value of the "out" JspWriter prior to pushing a BodyJspWriter. getPreviousOut() has no parameters and throws no exceptions.

Returns

- JspWriter

getTagData() Method

```
public TagData getTagData()
```

This method returns the immutable TagData for this tag. getTagData() has no parameters and throws no exceptions.

Returns

- TagData

getTagId() Method

```
public java.lang.String getTagId()
```

This method returns the value of the id or null for the Tag. getTagID() has no parameters and throws no exceptions.

Returns

- java.lang.String

getTagName() Method

```
public java.lang.String getTagName()
```

This method returns the short name for the Tag. getTagName() has no parameters and throws no exceptions.

Returns

- java.lang.String

getValue() Method

```
public java.lang.Object getValue(java.lang.String key)
```

This method returns the value associated with the tag. getValue() throws no exceptions.

Parameters

- java.lang.Object

Returns

- java.lang.String

initialize() Method

```
public void initialize(Tag parent,
    TagData tagData,
    PageContext pc)
```

This method initializes a `Tag` instance so it can be used or reused. A newly created `Tag` instance has to be prepared by invoking this method before invoking `doStartTag()`. A `Tag` instance that has been used and released by invoking `release()` must be reinitialized by invoking this method. `initialize()` returns no value and throws no exceptions.

Parameters

* `Tag`
* `TagData`
* `PageContext`

release() Method

```
public void release()
```

This method releases a `Tag` instance so it can be used or reused. `release()` has no parameters, returns no value, and throws no exceptions.

setBodyOut() Method

```
public void setBodyOut(BodyJspWriter b)
```

This method sets the `BodyJspWriter`. It will be invoked once per action invocation at most. It will not be invoked if there is no body evaluation. `setBodyOut()` returns no value and throws no exceptions.

Parameters

* `BodyJspWriter`

setValue() Method

```
public void setValue(java.lang.String key,
    java.lang.Object value)
```

This method sets a user-defined value on the `Tag`. `setValue()` returns no value and throws no exceptions.

Parameters

* `java.lang.String`
* `java.lang.Object`

TagAttributeInfo Class

```
public class TagAttributeInfo extends java.lang.Object
```

This class encapsulates information on `Tag` attributes. It is instantiated from the Tag Library Descriptor file (TLD). `TagAttributeInfo` class has three fields and four methods, described in the following sections.

ID Field

```
public static final java.lang.String ID
```

This field holds a reference to the tag's ID.

name Field

```
private java.lang.String name
```

This field holds a reference to the tag's short name.

reqTime Field

```
private boolean reqTime
```

This field holds a reference to the tag's request time.

setValue() Method

```
setValue(java.lang.String name,
    java.lang.String type,
    boolean reqTime)
```

This method is the constructor for `TagAttributeInfo`. There is no public constructor. This class is to be instantiated only from the tag library code under request from some JSP code that is parsing a TLD (Tag Library Descriptor). `setValue()` returns no value and throws no exceptions.

Parameters

- `java.lang.String`
- `java.lang.String`
- `boolean`

getIdAttribute() Method

```
public static TagAttributeInfo getIdAttribute(TagAttributeInfo[] a)
```

This method is a convenience method that goes through an array of `TagAttributeInfo` objects and looks for "id". `getIdAttribute()` throws no exceptions.

Parameters

- `TagAttributeInfo[]`

Returns

- `TagAttributeInfo`

getName() Method

`public java.lang.String getName()`

This method returns the name of the attribute for the `Tag`. `getName()` has no parameters and throws no exceptions.

Returns

- `java.lang.String`

getTypeName() Method

`public java.lang.String getTypeName()`

This method returns the type of the attribute for the `Tag`. `getTypeName()` has no parameters and throws no exceptions.

Returns

- `java.lang.String`

TagData Class

```
public class TagData extends java.lang.Object
    implements java.lang.Cloneable
```

This class encapsulates `Tag` instance attributes and values. Often, this data is fully static in the case where none of the attributes have runtime expressions as their values. Thus this class is intended to expose an immutable interface to a set of immutable attribute/value pairs. This class implements `Cloneable`, so that implementations can create a static instance and then just clone it before adding the request-time expressions. The `TagData` class has two fields and five methods, described in the following sections.

attributes Field

`private java.util.Hashtable attributes`

This field holds a reference to a `Hashtable` of the tag's attributes.

REQUEST_TIME_VALUE Field

`public static final java.lang.Object REQUEST_TIME_VALUE`

This field holds a reference to a distinguished value for an attribute. The value is a request-time expression, which is not yet available because this `TagData` instance is being used at translation-time.

TagData() Method

`public TagData(java.lang.Object[][] atts)`

This method is the constructor for a `TagData` object. It takes a single parameter, a two-dimensional array of static attributes and values. `TagData()` returns no values and throws no exceptions.

Parameters

- `java.lang.Object[][]`

getAttribute() Method

`public java.lang.Object getAttribute(java.lang.String name)`

This method returns the passed-in name's value. `getAttribute()` throws no exceptions.

Parameters

- `java.lang.String`

Returns

- `java.lang.Object`

getAttributeString() Method

`public java.lang.String getAttributeString(java.lang.String name)`

This method returns the value of an attribute as a `java.lang.String`. `getAttributeString()` throws no exceptions.

Parameters

- `java.lang.String`

Returns

- `java.lang.String`

getId() Method

`public java.lang.String getId()`

This method returns the value of the id attribute or null. `getID()` has no parameters and throws no exceptions.

Returns

- `java.lang.String`

setAttribute() Method

```
public void setAttribute(java.lang.String name,
    java.lang.Object value)
```

This method sets the value of an attribute/value pair. `setAttribute()` returns no value and throws no exceptions.

Parameters

- `java.lang.String`
- `java.lang.Object`

TagExtraInfo Class

```
public abstract class TagExtraInfo extends java.lang.Object
```

This class provides extra tag information for a custom tag. It is mentioned in the Tag Library Descriptor file (TLD). This class must be used if the tag defines any scripting variables, or if the tag wants to provide translation-time validation of the tag attributes. The TagExtraInfo class has one field and five methods, described in the following sections.

tagInfo Field

```
protected TagInfo tagInfo
```

This field holds a reference to the TagInfo object.

TagExtraInfo() Method

```
public TagExtraInfo()
```

This method is the default empty constructor for the TagExtraInfo class. TagExtraInfo() has no parameters, returns no value, and throws no exceptions.

getTagInfo() Method

```
public TagInfo getTagInfo()
```

This method returns the TagInfo object for this class. getTagInfo() has no parameters and throws no exceptions.

Returns

- TagInfo

getVariableInfo() Method

```
public VariableInfo[] getVariableInfo(TagData data)
```

This method returns information on scripting variables defined by this tag. getVariableInfo() throws no exceptions.

Parameters

- TagData

Returns

- VariableInfo[]

isValid() Method

```
public boolean isValid(TagData data)
```

This method performs translation-time validation of the TagData attributes, returning a boolean value indicating validity. isValid() throws no exceptions.

Parameters

- TagData

Returns

- boolean

setTagInfo() Method

```
public void setTagInfo(TagInfo info)
```

This method sets the `TagInfo` object for this class. `setTagInfo()` returns no value and throws no exceptions.

Parameters

- TagInfo

TagInfo Class

```
public abstract class TagInfo extends java.lang.Object
```

This class provides `Tag` information for a tag in a tag library. It is instantiated from the Tag Library Descriptor file (TLD). The TagInfo class has nine fields and eleven methods, described in the following sections.

attributeInfo Field

```
private TagAttributeInfo[] attributeInfo
```

This field holds a reference to an array of `TagAttributeInfo` objects.

BODY_CONTENT_JSP Field

```
public static final java.lang.String BODY_CONTENT_JSP
```

This field holds a reference to a static constant for `getBodyContent()`, when it is a JSP.

BODY_CONTENT_TAG_DEPENDENT Field

```
public static final java.lang.String BODY_CONTENT_TAG_DEPENDENT
```

This field holds a reference to a static constant for `getBodyContent()`, when it is `Tag` dependent.

bodyContent Field

```
private java.lang.String bodyContent
```

This field holds a reference to a `java.lang.String` containing information on the body content of these tags.

infoString Field

```
private java.lang.String infoString
```

This field holds a reference to a java.lang.String containing the optional string information for this tag.

tagClassName Field

```
private java.lang.String tagClassName
```

This field holds a reference to a java.lang.String containing the name of the tag handler class.

tagExtraInfo Field

```
private TagExtraInfo tagExtraInfo
```

This field holds a reference to an instance providing extra tag info.

tagLibrary Field

```
private TagLibraryInfo tagLibrary
```

This field holds a reference to an instance of the tag library that contains this tag.

tagName Field

```
private java.lang.String tagName
```

This field holds a reference to a java.lang.String containing the name of this tag.

TagInfo() Method

```
public TagInfo(java.lang.String tagName,
    java.lang.String tagClassName,
    java.lang.String bodycontent,
    java.lang.String infoString,
    TagLibraryInfo tagLib,
    TagExtraInfo tagExtraInfo,
    TagAttributeInfo[] attribInfo)
```

This method is the constructor for TagInfo. There is no public constructor. This class is to be instantiated only from the tag library code under request from some JSP code that is parsing a TLD (Tag Library Descriptor). TagInfo() returns no value and throws no exceptions.

Parameters

- java.lang.String
- java.lang.String
- java.lang.String
- java.lang.String
- TagLibraryInfo

- TagExtraInfo
- TagAttributeInfo[]

getAttributes() Method

public TagAttributeInfo[] getAttributes()

This method returns a reference to an array of TagAttributeInfo objects. If a null is returned, then there is no attribute information. getAttributes() has no parameters and throws no exceptions.

Returns

- TagAttributeInfo[]

getBodyContent() Method

public java.lang.String getBodyContent()

This method returns a reference to a java.lang.String containing information on the body content of these tags. getBody Content() has no parameters and throws no exceptions.

Returns

- java.lang.String

getInfoString() Method

public java.lang.String getInfoString()

This method returns a reference to a java.lang.String containing the optional string information for this tag. getInfoString() has no parameters and throws no exceptions.

Returns

- java.lang.String

getTagClassName() Method

public java.lang.String getTagClassName()

This method returns a reference to a java.lang.String containing the name of the tag handler class. getTagClassName() has no parameters and throws no exceptions.

Returns

- java.lang.String

getTagExtraInfo() Method

public TagExtraInfo getTagExtraInfo()

This method returns a reference to the TagExtraInfo object. getTagExtraInfo() has no parameters and throws no exceptions.

Returns

- TagExtraInfo

getTagLibrary() Method

`public TagLibraryInfo getTagLibrary()`

This method returns a reference to the `TagLibraryInfo` object. `getTagLibrary()` has no parameters and throws no exceptions.

Returns

- TagLibraryInfo

getTagName() Method

`public java.lang.String getTagName()`

This method returns a reference to a `java.lang.String` containing the name of this tag. `getTagName()` has no parameters and throws no exceptions.

Returns

- java.lang.String

getVariableInfo() Method

`public VariableInfo[] getVariableInfo(TagData data)`

This method returns information on the object created by this tag at runtime. If null is returned, then no such object was created. The default is null if the tag has no `id` attribute. `getVariableInfo()` throws no exceptions.

Parameters

- TagData

Returns

- VariableInfo[]

isValid() Method

`public boolean isValid(TagData data)`

This method performs translation-time validation of the `TagData` attributes. `isValid()` throws no exceptions.

Parameters

- TagData

Returns

- boolean

TagLibraryInfo Class

`public abstract class TagLibraryInfo extends java.lang.Object`

This class provides information on the tag library. It is instantiated from the Tag Library Descriptor file (TLD). `TagLibraryInfo` class has three fields and nine methods.

prefix Field

`private java.lang.String prefix`

This field holds a reference to the prefix actually used by the `taglib` directive.

tldis Field

`protected java.io.InputStream tldis`

This field holds a reference to the input stream to the TLD.

uri Field

`private java.net.URL uri`

This field holds a reference to the URI actually used by the taglib directive.

TagLibraryInfo() Method

```
public TagLibraryInfo(java.lang.String prefix,
    java.net.URL uri,
    java.io.InputStream tldis)
```

This method is the constructor for the `TagLibraryInfo` class. It will invoke the constructors for `TagInfo` and `TagAttributeInfo` after parsing the TLD file. `TagLibraryInfo()` returns no value and throws no exceptions.

Parameters

- `java.lang.String`
- `java.net.URL`
- `java.io.InputStream`

getInfoString() Method

`public java.lang.String getInfoString()`

This method returns the information string for this tag library. `getInfoString()` has no parameters and throws no exceptions.

Returns

- `java.lang.String`

getPrefixString() Method

`public java.lang.String getPrefixString()`

This method returns the prefix assigned to this taglib from the taglib directive. `getPrefixString()` has no parameters and throws no exceptions.

Returns

- `java.lang.String`

getReliableURN() Method

`public java.lang.String getReliableURN()`

This method returns a reliable URN to a TLD. `getReliableURN()` has no parameters and throws no exceptions.

Returns

- `java.lang.String`

getRequiredVersion() Method

`public java.lang.String getRequiredVersion()`

This method returns the required version for the taglib. `getRequiredVersion()` has no parameters and throws no exceptions.

Returns

- `java.lang.String`

getShortName() Method

`public java.lang.String getShortName()`

This method returns the preferred short name for the taglib. `getShortName()` has no parameters and throws no exceptions.

Returns

- `java.lang.String`

getTag() Method

`public TagInfo getTag(java.lang.String name)`

This method returns the `TagInfo` for a given tag short name. `getTag()` throws no exceptions.

Parameters

- `java.lang.String`

Returns

- `TagInfo`

getTags() Method

```
public TagInfo[] getTags()
```

This method returns an array of `TagInfo` objects for the tags defined in this tag library. `getTags()` has no parameters and throws no exceptions.

Returns

- `TagInfo[]`

getURI() Method

```
public java.net.URL getURI()
```

This method returns the URI from the "<%@" taglib directive for this library. `getURI()` has no parameters and throws no exceptions.

Returns

- `java.net.URL`

VariableInfo Class

```
public class VariableInfo extends java.lang.Object
```

This class provides information on the scripting variables that are created and modified by a tag at runtime. This information is provided by `TagExtraInfo` classes and it is used by the translation phase of JSP. `VariableInfo` class has seven fields and five methods, described in the following sections.

AT_BEGIN Field

```
public static final int AT_BEGIN
```

This field states that the visibility of a variable begins after the start tag.

AT_END Field

```
public static final int AT_END
```

This field states that the visibility of a variable begins after the end tag.

className Field

```
private java.lang.String className
```

This field holds a reference to the name of the scripting variable.

declare Field

```
private boolean declare
```

This field determines if the variable is a new variable.

NESTED Field

```
public static final int NESTED
```

This field states that the visibility of a variable is between the start and end tags.

scope Field

```
private int scope
```

This field indicates the lexical scope of the variable.

varName Field

```
private java.lang.String varName
```

This field represents the name of the scripting variable.

VariableInfo() Method

```
public VariableInfo(java.lang.String varName,
    java.lang.String className,
    boolean declare,
    int scope)
```

This method is the `VariableInfo` constructor. These objects can be created at translation time by the `TagExtraInfo` instances. `VariableInfo()` returns no value and throws no exceptions.

Parameters

- `java.lang.String`
- `java.lang.String`
- `boolean`
- `int`

getClassName() Method

```
public java.lang.String getClassName()
```

This method returns the class name of the scripting variable. `getClassName()` has no parameters and throws no exceptions.

Returns

- `java.lang.String`

getDeclare() Method

```
public boolean getDeclare()
```

This method returns a `boolean` that indicates whether the variable is a new variable. `getDeclare()` has no parameters and throws no exceptions.

Returns

- `boolean`

getScope() Method

`public int getScope()`

This method returns an integer indicating the lexical scope of the variable. `getScope()` has no parameters and throws no exceptions.

Returns

- `int`

getVarName() Method

`public java.lang.String getVarName()`

This method returns to the class name of the scripting variable. `getVarName()` has no parameters and throws no exceptions.

Returns

- `java.lang.String`

CHAPTER 20

The javax.servlet Package

The java.servlet package is at the core of all servlet development. It contains the generic interfaces, classes, and exceptions that are implemented and extended by all servlets. Figure 20.1 contains the javax.servlet object model.

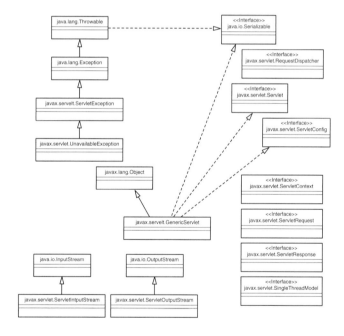

Figure 20.1

The javax.servlet *object model.*

javax.servlet Interfaces

Interfaces of the javax.servlet package include RequestDispatcher, Servlet, ServletConfig, ServletContext, ServletRequest, ServletResponse, and SingleThreadModel. Each is described in the following sections, along with its methods.

RequestDispatcher Interface

```
public interface RequestDispatcher
```

The RequestDispatcher interface defines an object, which can serve as a wrapper around another resource on the server. It is most often used to forward requests to other server resources. It defines two methods.

forward() Method

```
public void forward(ServletRequest request,
  ServletResponse response)
  throws ServletException,
  java.io.IOException
```

The forward() method is used for forwarding a request from one servlet to another. It allows the first servlet to perform some initial tasks on the request before forwarding it to another resource on the server. forward() returns no value.

Parameters

- ServletRequest
- ServletResponse

Exceptions Thrown

- ServletException
- java.io.IOException

include() Method

```
public void include(ServletRequest request,
  ServletResponse response)
  throws ServletException,
  java.io.IOException
```

The include() method is used to merge content from another server resource in the response of the final servlet. include() returns no value.

Parameters

- ServletRequest
- ServletResponse

Exceptions Thrown

- ServletException
- java.io.IOException

Servlet Interface

```
public abstract interface Servlet
```

The `Servlet` interface is implemented by all servlets either through direct implementation or inheritance. It defines five methods, including the three life cycle methods, to be implemented by all servlets.

init() Method

```
public void init(ServletConfig config)
   throws ServletException
```

The `init()` method, being the first life cycle method, marks the beginning of a servlet's life. It is called only when the servlet is first loaded, and it must execute successfully before the servlet can service requests. The `init()` method should contain all initialization code for the servlet. It returns no value.

Parameters

- `ServletConfig`

Exceptions Thrown

- `ServletException`

getServletConfig() Method

```
public ServletConfig getServletConfig()
```

The `getServletConfig()` method returns the servlet's `ServletConfig` object, which contains the servlet's startup configuration and initialization parameters. `getServletConfig()` has no parameters and throws no exceptions.

Returns

- `ServletConfig`

service() Method

```
public void service(ServletRequest request,
   ServletResponse response)
   throws ServletException,
   java.io.IOException
```

The `service()` method defines the servlet's entry point for servicing requests. It can be executed only after the servlet's `init()` method has executed successfully. The `service()` method is the life cycle method executed for every incoming request. It returns no value.

Parameters

- `ServletRequest`
- `ServletResponse`

Exceptions Thrown

- ServletException
- java.io.IOException

getServletInfo() Method

`public java.lang.String getServletinfo()`

The getServletInfo() method is used to provide the servlet user with information about the servlet itself. You will usually include copyright or versioning information. getServletInfo() has no parameters and throws no exceptions.

Returns

- String

destroy() Method

`public void destroy()`

The destroy() method is the life cycle method that marks the end of a servlet's life. It is executed only once when the servlet is removed from the service. You should place all your clean-up functionality in this method. destroy() has no parameters, returns no value, and throws no exceptions.

ServletConfig Interface

The ServletConfig interface defines an object generated by a servlet engine and is used to pass configuration information to a servlet during start up. It contains name/value pairs of initialization parameters for the servlet. It also contains a reference to the ServletContext object, which is described in the next section. The ServletConfig interface defines four methods for accessing this information.

getServletContext() Method

`public ServletContext getServletContext()`

The getServletContext() method returns a reference to the current ServletContext object. getServletContext() has no parameters and throws no exceptions.

Returns

- ServletContext

getServletName() Method

`public java.lang.String getServletName()`

The getServletName() method returns the registered servlet's name. getServletName() has no parameters and throws no exceptions.

Returns

- java.lang.String

getInitParameter() Method

```
public java.lang.String getInitParameter(java.lang.String)
```

The getInitParameter() method returns a String containing the value of the initialization parameter's name/value pair referenced by the passed in String representing the name. getInitParameter() throws no exceptions.

Parameters

- java.lang.String

Returns

- java.lang.String

getInitParameterNames() Method

```
public java.util.Enumeration getInitParameterNames()
```

The getInitParameterNames() method returns an Enumeration of Strings representing all of the initialization parameters' names. getInitParameterNames() takes no parameters and throws no exceptions.

Returns

- java.util.Enumeration

ServletContext Interface

```
public interface ServletContext
```

The ServletContext interface defines an object, to be created by a servlet engine, that contains information about the servlet's environment. This interface provides several methods to access this information.

getContext() Method

```
public ServletContext getContext(java.lang.String uripath)
```

The getContext() method returns a reference to a ServletContext object belonging to a particular URI path. getContext() throws no exceptions.

Parameters

- java.lang.String

Returns

- ServletContext

getInitParameter() Method

```
public java.lang.String getInitParameter(java.lang.String name)
```

The getInitParameter() method returns the value for the named context parameter. getInitParameter() throws no exceptions.

Parameters

- `java.lang.String`

Returns

- `java.lang.String`

getInitParameterNames() Method

`public Enumeration getInitParameterNames()`

The `getInitParameterNames()` method returns an `Enumeration` of all the context parameter names. `getInitParameterNames()` has no parameters and throws no exceptions.

Returns

- `Enumeration`

getMajorVersion() Method

`public int getMajorVersion()`

The `getMajorVersion()` method returns an integer representing the major version of the servlet API that the servlet engine supports. If the servlet engine supported the servlet API 2.1, the result would be 2. `getMajorVersion()` has no parameters and throws no exceptions.

Returns

- `int`

getMinorVersion() Method

`public int getMinorVersion()`

The `getMinorVersion()` method returns an integer representing the minor version of the servlet API that the servlet engine supports. If the servlet engine supported the servlet API 2.1, the result would be 1. `getMinorVersion()` has no parameters and throws no exceptions.

Returns

- `int`

getMimeType() Method

`public java.lang.String getMimeType(java.lang.String file)`

The `getMimeType()` method returns a `String` representing the MIME type of the passed in file name, or null if the MIME type of the file is not known. `getMimeType()` throws no exceptions.

Parameters

- `java.lang.String`

Returns

- java.lang.String

getNamedDispatcher() Method

```
public RequestDispatcher getNamedDispatcher(java.lang.String name)
```

The getNamedDispatcher() method returns a reference to a RequestDispatcher object belonging to a particular URI path. The getNamedDispatcher() method throws no exceptions.

Parameters

- java.lang.String

Returns

- RequestDispatcher

getResource() Method

```
public java.net.URL getResource(java.lang.String path)
    throws java.net.MalformedURLException
```

The getResource() method returns a URL object of a resource matching the passed in path parameter, permitting a servlet to access content from the servlet engine's document space without system dependencies.

Parameters

- java.lang.String

Returns

- java.net.URL

Exceptions Thrown

- java.net.MalformedURLException

getResourceAsStream() Method

```
public java.io.InputStream
    getResourceAsStream(java.lang.String path)
```

The getResourceAsStream() method returns an InputStream object, which allows access to the resource matching the passed in URL path. getResourceAsStream() throws no exceptions.

Parameters

- java.lang.String

Returns

- java.io.InputStream

getRequestDispatcher() Method

```
public RequestDispatcher
  getRequestDispatcher(java.lang.String urlpath)
```

The getRequestDispatcher() method returns a RequestDispatcher object based on the passed in URL path. getRequestDispatcher() throws no exceptions.

Parameters

- java.lang.String

Returns

- RequestDispatcher

log(java.lang.String msg) Method

```
public void log(java.lang.String msg)
```

The log() method writes the passed in message to the context's log. The location of the log is servlet engine specific. log() returns no value and throws no exceptions.

Parameters

- java.lang.String

log(java.lang.String msg, java.lang.Throwable throwable) Method

```
public void log(java.lang.String msg,
  java.lang.Throwable throwable)
```

This log() method writes the passed in message and the stack trace of the passed in Throwable object to the context's log. The location of the log is servlet engine specific. log() returns no value and throws no exceptions.

Parameters

- java.lang.String
- java.lang.Throwable

getRealPath() Method

```
public java.lang.String getRealPath(java.lang.String path)
```

The getRealPath() method returns a String representing the passed in virtual path converted to the real path based on the operating system that the servlet engine is running on. getRealPath() throws no exceptions.

Parameters

- java.lang.String

Returns

- java.lang.String

getServer Info() Method

`public java.lang.String getServerInfo()`

The `getServerInfo()` method returns a `String` representing the name and version of the server that the servlet is running under. If the servlet was running under the Java Web Server 1.1.3, then the returned String would be Java Web Server/1.1.3. `getRealPath()` has no parameters and throws no exceptions.

Returns

- java.lang.String

getAttribute() Method

`public java.lang.Object getAttribute(java.lang.String name)`

The `getAttribute()` method returns an `Object` stored in the `ServletContext` and keyed by the name value passed in. This is one of methods used to share resources between servlets. The returning object must be downcast to its original type before use. `getAttribute()` throws no exceptions.

Parameters

- java.lang.String

Returns

- java.lang.Object

getAttributeNames() Method

`public java.util.Enumeration getAttributeNames()`

The `getAttributeNames()` method returns an `Enumeration` of `Strings` representing the names of the attributes currently stored in the `ServletContext`. `getAttributeNames()` has no parameters and throws no exceptions.

Returns

- java.util.Enumeration

setAttribute() Method

`public void setAttribute(java.lang.String name,`
`  java.lang.Object)`

The `setAttribute()` method stores an `Object` in the `ServletContext` and binds the `Object` to the given name. If the name already exists in the `ServletContext`, then it is replaced. `setAttribute()` returns no value and throws no exceptions.

Parameters

- java.lang.String
- java.lang.Object

removeAttribute() Method

`public void removeAttribute(java.lang.String name)`

The `removeAttribute()` method removes the `Object`, which is bound to the passed in name, from the `ServletContext`. `removeAttribute()` returns no value and throws no exceptions.

Parameters

- `java.lang.String`

ServletRequest Interface

`public interface ServletRequest`

The `ServletRequest` interface defines an object used to encapsulate information about the client's request. Information in the `ServletRequest` object includes parameter name/value pairs, attributes, and an input stream. The `ServletRequest` interface defines the following methods to access this information.

getAttribute() Method

`public java.lang.Object getAttribute(java.lang.String name)`

The `getAttribute()` method returns the value of the object keyed by the name string for the current request. `getAttribute()` throws no exceptions.

Parameters

- `java.lang.String`

Returns

- `java.lang.Object`

getAttributeNames() Method

`public java.util.Enumeration getAttributeNames()`

The `getAttributeNames()` method returns an `Enumeration` containing the names of all the attributes in the current request. `getAttributeNames()` has no parameters and throws no exceptions.

Returns

- `java.util.Enumeration`

getCharacterEncoding() Method

`public java.lang.String getCharacterEncoding()`

The `getCharacterEncoding()` method returns a `String` representing the character set encoding for this request. `getCharacterEncoding()` has no parameters and throws no exceptions.

Returns

- `java.lang.String`

getContentLength() Method

`public int getContentLength()`

The `getContentLength()` method returns an integer value equal to the length of the request's data. It is equivalent to the CGI variable `CONTENT_LENGTH`. `getContentLength()` has no parameters and throws no exceptions.

Returns

- `int`

getContentType() Method

`public java.lang.String getContentType()`

The `getContentType()` method returns a `String` representing the MIME type of the request's data. It is equivalent to the CGI variable `CONTENT_TYPE`. `getContentLength()` has no parameters and throws no exceptions.

Returns

- `java.lang.String`

getInputStream() Method

`public ServletInputStream getInputStream()`
`  throws java.io.IOException`

The `getInputStream()` method returns an input stream for reading binary data from the request's body. `getInputStream()` has no parameters.

Returns

- `ServletInputStream`

Exceptions Thrown

- `java.io.IOException`

getLocale() Method

`public Locale getLocale()`

The `getLocale()` method returns the client's most preferred locale. `getLocale()` has no parameters and throws no exceptions.

Returns

- `Locale`

getLocales() Method

`public Enumeration getLocales()`

The getLocales() method returns an Enumeration containing the client's most preferred Locale objects. getLocales() has no parameters and throws no exceptions.

Returns

- Enumeration

getParameter() Method

```
public java.lang.String getParameter(java.lang.String name)
```

The getParameter() method returns the value of the requested parameter. If the parameter has or could have more than one value, use the getParameterValues() method. getParameter() throws no exceptions.

Parameters

- java.lang.String

Returns

- java.lang.String

getParameterNames() Method

```
public java.util.Enumeration getParameterNames()
```

The getParameterNames() method returns an Enumeration of Strings representing the parameter names for this request. getParameterNames() has no parameters and throws no exceptions.

Returns

- java.util.Enumeration

getParameterValues() Method

```
public java.lang.String[] getParameterValues(java.lang.String name)
```

The getParameterValues() method returns an array of Strings representing all of the values for the named parameter in the current request. getParameterValues() throws no exceptions.

Parameters

- java.lang.String

Returns

- java.lang.String[]

getProtocol() Method

```
public java.lang.String getProtocol()
```

The getProtocol() method returns a String representing the protocol and version of the request. It is the same as the CGI variable SERVER_PROTOCOL. getProtocol() has no parameters and throws no exceptions.

Returns

- `java.lang.String`

getRequestDispatcher() Method

`public RequestDispatcher getRequestDispatcher(java.lang.String path)`

The `getRequestDispatcher()` method returns a `RequestDispatcher` object using a relative path. `getRequestDispatcher()` throws no exceptions.

Parameters

- `java.lang.String`

Returns

- `RequestDispatcher`

getScheme() Method

`public java.lang.String getScheme()`

The `getScheme()` method returns a `String` representing the scheme of the URL used in the request. Sample schemes include http, https, and ftp. `getScheme()` has no parameters and throws no exceptions.

Returns

- `java.lang.String`

getServerName() Method

`public java.lang.String getServerName()`

The `getServerName()` method returns a `String` representing the hostname of the server that received the request. It is the same as the CGI variable SERVER_NAME. `getServerName()` has no parameters and throws no exceptions.

Returns

- `java.lang.String`

getServerPort() Method

`public int getServerPort()`

The `getServerPort()` method returns an integer representing the port number on which the request was received. It is the same as the CGI variable SERVER_PORT. `getServerPort()` has no parameters and throws no exceptions.

Returns

- `int`

getReader() Method

`public java.io.BufferedReader getReader()`
`  throws java.io.IOException`

The getReader() method returns a BufferedReader for reading text input from the request body. getReader() has no parameters.

Returns

- java.io.BufferedReader

Exceptions Thrown

- java.io.IOException

getRemoteAddress() Method

`public java.lang.String getRemoteAddress()`

The getRemoteAddress() method returns a String representing the IP address of the client sending the request. It is the same as the CGI variable REMOTE_ADDR. getRemoteAddress() has no parameters and throws no exceptions.

Returns

- java.lang.String

getRemoteHost() Method

`public java.lang.String getRemoteHost()`

The getRemoteHost() method returns a String representing the qualified hostname of the client sending the request. It is the same as the CGI variable REMOTE_HOST. getRemoteHost() has no parameters and throws no exceptions.

Returns

- java.lang.String

isSecure() Method

`public boolean isSecure()`

The isSecure() method returns a boolean value indicating whether or not the request was made with a secure channel. isSecure() has no parameters and throws no exceptions.

Returns

- boolean

removeAttribute() Method

`public void removeAttribute(java.lang.String name)`

The removeAttribute() method removes the named attribute from the ServletRequest. removeAttribute() returns no value and throws no exceptions.

Parameters

- java.lang.String

setAttribute() Method

```
public void setAttribute(java.lang.String key,
  java.lang.Object object) throws IllegalStateException
```

The setAttribute() method adds an attribute to the request's context keyed by the passed in key String. It throws a IllegalStateException, if the key already exists. setAttribute() returns no value.

Parameters

- java.lang.String
- java.lang.Object

Exceptions Thrown

- IllegalStateException

ServletResponse Interface

```
public interface ServletResponse
```

The ServletResponse interface defines an object for sending MIME data back to the client from the servlet's service method. The ServletResponse object is a parameter of the servlet's service method. The ServletResponse interface defines several methods for implementing objects.

flushBuffer() Method

```
public void flushBuffer()
  throws IOException
```

The flushBuffer() method flushes and commits the response. flushBuffer() has no parameters and returns no value.

Exceptions Thrown

- java.io.IOException

getBufferSize() Method

```
public int getBufferSize()
```

The getBufferSize() method returns the size of the response buffer. getBufferSize() has no parameters and throws no exceptions.

Returns

- int

getCharacterEncoding() Method

```
public java.lang.String getCharacterEncoding()
```

The getCharacterEncoding() method returns the character set encoding used for this request's body. If there has been no content type assigned, it is, by default, set to text/plain. getCharacterEncoding() has no parameters and throws no exceptions.

Returns

- java.lang.String

getLocale() Method

public Locale getLocale()

The getLocale() method returns the current response locale. getLocale() has no parameters and throws no exceptions.

Returns

- Locale

getOutputStream() Method

public ServletOutputStream getOutputStream()
  throws java.io.IOException

The getOutputStream() method returns an output stream used for writing binary data to the response. getOutputStream() has no parameters.

Returns

- ServletOutputStream

Exceptions Thrown

- java.io.IOException

getWriter() Method

public java.io.PrintWriter getWriter()
  throws java.io.IOException

The getWriter() method returns a print writer used for writing formatted text to the response object. getWriter() has no parameters.

Returns

- java.io.PrintWriter

Exceptions Thrown

- java.io.IOException

isCommitted() Method

public boolean isCommitted()

The isCommitted() method returns true if part of the response has already been sent. isCommitted() has no parameters and throws no exceptions.

Returns

- boolean

reset() Method

`public void reset()`

The `reset()` method empties the response buffer and clears the response headers. `reset()` has no parameters, returns no value, and throws no exceptions.

setBufferSize() Method

`public void setBufferSize(int size)`

The `setBufferSize()` method sets the size of the response buffer. `setBufferSize()` returns no value and throws no exceptions.

Parameters

- `int`

setContentLength() Method

`public void setContentLength(int len)`

The `setContentLength()` method sets the content length of the current response. `setContentLength()` returns no value and throws no exceptions.

Parameters

- `int`

setContentType() Method

`public void setContentType(java.lang.String type)`

The `setContentType()` method sets the content type of the current response. You can only set this property once for the current response. This method must be called before calling the `getWriter()` or `getOutputStream()` methods. `setContentType()` returns no value and throws no exceptions.

Parameters

- `java.lang.String`

setLocale() Method

`public void setLocale(Locale locale)`

The `setLocale()` method sets the response locale, including headers and character sets. `setLocale()` returns no value and throws no exceptions.

Parameters

- `Locale`

SingleThreadModel Interface

`public interface SingleThreadModel`

The `SingleThreadModel` interface defines a single threaded model for the implementing servlet's execution. Implementing this interface makes the servlet thread safe. This guarantees that the implementing servlet's service method will not be executed concurrently by more than one thread. There are no methods defined by the `SingleThreadModel` interface.

Classes

Classes for the `javax.servlet` package are `GenericServlet`, `ServletInputStream`, and `ServletOutputStream`. Their methods are described in the following sections.

GenericServlet Class

The `GenericServlet` class was created to provide a basic foundation of new servlets. It provides default life cycle methods and default implementations of the `ServletConfig`'s methods.

GenericServlet() Method

```
public GenericServlet()
```

The `GenericServlet()` method is an empty default constructor. `GenericServlet()` has no parameters, returns no value, and throws no exceptions.

destroy() Method

```
public void destroy()
```

The `destroy()` method is executed when the servlet is removed from the running service. It performs any cleanup of resources that were allocated in the `init()` method. `destroy()` has no parameters, returns no value, and throws no exceptions.

getInitParameter() Method

```
public java.lang.String getInitParameter(
  java.lang.String name)
```

The `getInitParameter()` method returns a `String` containing the value of the initialization parameter keyed by the passed in name. `getInitParameter()` throws no exceptions.

Parameters

- `java.lang.String`

Returns

- `java.lang.String`

getInitParameterNames() Method

```
public java.util.Enumeration getInitParameterNames()
```

The getInitParameterNames() method returns an Enumeration containing all of the names for each initialization parameter. getInitParameterNames() has no parameters and throws no exceptions.

Returns

* java.util.Enumeration

getServletConfig() Method

public ServletConfig getServletConfig()

The getServletConfig() method returns a ServletConfig object containing any startup configuration information for this servlet. getServletConfig() has no parameters and throws no exceptions.

Returns

* ServletConfig

getServletContext() Method

public ServletContext getServletContext()

The getServletContext() method returns a ServletContext object containing information about the servlet's network service. getServletContext() has no parameters and throws no exceptions.

Returns

* ServletContext

getServletInfo() Method

public java.lang.String getServletInfo()

The getServletInfo() method returns a String containing servlet-specific information about the implementing servlet. getServletInfo() has no parameters and throws no exceptions.

Returns

* java.lang.String

init(ServletConfig config) Method

public void init(ServletConfig config)
  throws ServletException

The init() method marks the beginning of a servlet's life. It is called only when the servlet is first loaded, and it must execute successfully before the servlet can service requests. The init() method should contain all initialization code for the servlet. It returns no value.

Parameters

- ServletConfig (encapsulates the servlet's startup configuration and initialization parameters)

Exceptions Thrown

- ServletException

init() Method

```
public void init()
  throws ServletException
```

This parameterless implementation of the init() method is provided only for convenience. It prevents a derived servlet from having to store the ServletConfig object. init() has no parameters and returns no value.

Exceptions Thrown

- ServletException

log(java.lang.String message) Method

```
public void log(java.lang.String message)
```

The log() method takes the passed in message and the name of the servlet and writes them to a log file. The location of the log is server specific. log() returns no value and throws no exceptions.

Parameters

- java.lang.String

log(java.lang.String message, java.lang.Throwable t) Method

```
public void log(java.lang.String message,
  java.lang.Throwable t)
```

This log() method takes the passed in message and Throwable object and logs the message with a stack trace from the Throwable object. log() returns no value and throws no exceptions.

Parameters

- java.lang.String
- java.lang.Throwable

service() Method

```
public void service(ServletRequest request,
  ServletResponse response)
  throws ServletException,
  java.io.IOException
```

The `service()` method defines the servlet's entry point for servicing requests. It can be executed only after the servlet's `init()` method has executed successfully. The `service()` method is the life cycle method executed for every incoming request. It returns no value.

Parameters

- `ServletRequest`
- `ServletResponse`

Exceptions Thrown

- `ServletException`
- `java.io.IOException`

ServletInputStream Class

The `ServletInputStream` is an abstract class defined for servlet writers to get data from the client. It is meant to be implemented by a network services writer. This class has two methods.

ServletInputStream() Method

```
protected ServletInputStream()
```

The `ServletInputStream()` method is the empty default constructor. It has no parameters, returns no value, and throws no exceptions.

readLine() Method

```
public void readLine(byte[] b,
   int off,
   int len)
   throws java.io.IOException
```

The `readLine()` method reads the `len` of bytes into the passed in byte array `b`, starting at position `off`. If the character `'\n'` is encountered, then no more bytes are read in. `readLine()` returns no value.

Parameters

- `byte[]`
- `int`
- `int`

Exceptions Thrown

- `java.io.IOException`

ServletOutputStream Class

The `ServletOutputStream` class is used to write responses back to the client. It is an abstract class that is implemented by the network services implementor. To access the `ServletOutputStream`, you must call the `ServletResponse`'s `getOutputStream()` method. The class has several methods.

ServletOutputStream() Method

```
public ServletOutputStream()
  throws java.io.IOException
```

The `ServletOutputStream()` method is the empty default constructor. It has no parameters and returns no value.

Exceptions Thrown

- `java.io.IOException`

print(boolean value) Method

```
public void print(boolean value)
  throws java.io.IOException
```

This version of the `print()` method prints the passed in `boolean` value to the output stream.

Parameters

- `boolean`

> **NOTE**
>
> The print() method always throws a `java.io.IOException` exception. For all print values, the `print()` method returns no value.

print(char value) Method

```
public void print(char value)
  throws java.io.IOException
```

This version of the `print()` method prints the passed in `char` value to the output stream.

Parameters

- `char`

print(double value) Method

```
public void print(double value)
  throws java.io.IOException
```

This version of the `print()` method prints the passed in `double` value to the output stream.

Parameters

- `double`

print(float value) Method

```
public void print(float value)
  throws java.io.IOException
```

This version of the print() method prints the passed in float value to the output stream.

Parameters

- float

print(int value) Method

```
public void print(int value)
   throws java.io.IOException
```

This version of the print() method prints the passed in int value to the output stream.

Parameters

- int

print(long value) Method

```
public void print(long value)
   throws java.io.IOException
```

This version of the print() method prints the passed in long value to the output stream.

Parameters

- long

print(java.lang.String value) Method

```
public void print(java.lang.String value)
   throws java.io.IOException
```

This version of the print() method prints the passed in String value to the output stream.

Parameters

- java.lang.String

println() Method

```
public void println()
   throws java.io.IOException
```

This version of the println() method prints CRLF to the output stream and has no parameters.

NOTE

The println() method always throws a java.io.IOException exception. For all print values, the println() method returns no value.

println(java.lang.String value) Method

```
public void println(java.lang.String value)
  throws java.io.IOException
```

This version of the println() method prints the passed in String value to the output stream, followed by a CRLF.

Parameters

• java.lang.String

println(boolean value) Method

```
public void println(boolean value)
  throws java.io.IOException
```

This version of the println() method prints the passed in boolean value to the output stream, followed by a CRLF.

Parameters

• boolean

println(char value) Method

```
public void println(char value)
  throws java.io.IOException
```

This version of the println() method prints the passed in char value to the output stream, followed by a CRLF.

Parameters

• char

println(int value) Method

```
public void println(int value)
  throws java.io.IOException
```

This version of the println() method prints the passed in int value to the output stream, followed by a CRLF.

Parameters

• int

println(long value) Method

```
public void println(long value)
  throws java.io.IOException
```

This version of the println() method prints the passed in long value to the output stream, followed by a CRLF.

Parameters

- `long`

println(float value) Method

```
public void println(float value)
   throws java.io.IOException
```

This version of the `println()` method prints the passed in `float` value to the output stream, followed by a CRLF.

Parameters

- `float`

println(double value) Method

```
public void println(double value)
   throws java.io.IOException
```

This version of the `println()` method prints the passed in `double` value to the output stream, followed by a CRLF.

Parameters

- `double`

Exceptions

Exceptions for the `javax.servlet` package are `ServletException` and `UnavailableException`. Their methods are described in the following sections.

ServletException Exception

A `ServletException` object is thrown when a problem is encountered within a servlet.

ServletException() Method

```
public ServletException()
```

`ServletException()` method is the empty constructor. It has no parameters, returns no value, and throws no exceptions.

ServletException(java.lang.String message) Method

```
public ServletException(java.lang.String message)
```

Creates a new `ServletException` object with the passed in `String` as the message.

Parameters

- `java.lang.String`

NOTE

The `ServletException()` method always returns no value and throws no exceptions.

ServletException(java.lang.String message, java.lang.Throwable rootCause) Method

```
public ServletException(java.lang.String message,
  java.lang.Throwable rootCause)
```

Creates a ServletException object with a message and a Throwable object representing the cause of the exception.

Parameters

- java.lang.String
- java.lang.Throwable

ServletException() Method

```
public ServletException(java.lang.Throwable rootCause)
```

Creates a new ServletException object with a Throwable object representing the cause of the exception.

Parameters

- java.lang.Throwable

getRootCause() Method

```
public java.lang.Throwable getRootCause()
```

The getRootCause() method returns a Throwable object representing the cause of the exception. getRootCause() has no parameters and throws no exceptions.

Returns

- java.lang.Throwable

UnavailableException Exception

An UnavailableException is thrown when a servlet is not available to service a request. There are two types of UnavailableExceptions: permanent and temporary.

When a servlet is permanently unavailable, the servlet will not be able to service requests until some administrative task is completed.

When a servlet is temporarily unavailable, the servlet is expected to be able to service requests within a given period of time.

UnavailableException(Servlet servlet, java.lang.String msg) Method

```
public UnavailableException(Servlet servlet,
  java.lang.String msg)
```

This constructor creates a UnavailableException() with a reference to the servlet that is unavailable and a String representing the error message. This constructor creates an UnavailableException(), denoting permanent unavailability.

Parameters

- Servlet
- java.lang.String

UnavailableException(java.lang.String msg, int seconds) Method

public UnavailableException(java.lang.String msg, int seconds)

This constructor creates an UnavailableException() with an int value, representing an estimated time of unavailability. It also receives a reference to a String representing the error message.

Parameters

- java.lang.String
- int

UnavailableException(java.lang.String msg)Method

public UnavailableException(java.lang.String msg)

This constructor creates a UnavailableException() with a String representing the error message. This constructor creates an UnavailableException(), denoting permanent unavailability

Parameters

- java.lang.String

isPermanent() Method

public boolean isPermanent()

The isPermanent() method returns true if the servlet is permanently unavailable; otherwise, it returns false. isPermanent() has no parameters and throws no exceptions.

Returns

- boolean

getServlet() Method

public Servlet getServlet()

The getServlet() method returns a reference to the servlet that is reported as unavailable. getServlet() has no parameters and throws no exceptions.

Returns

- Servlet

getUnavailableSeconds() Method

```
public int getUnavailableSeconds()
```

The getUnavailableSeconds() method returns an int representing the number of seconds a servlet is expected to be temporarily unavailable. getUnavailableSeconds() has no parameters and throws no exceptions.

Returns

- int

CHAPTER 21

The javax.servlet.http Package

The java.servlet.http package contains the interfaces and classes that are implemented and extended, respectively, to create HTTP-specific servlets. Figure 21.1 contains the javax.servlet.http object model.

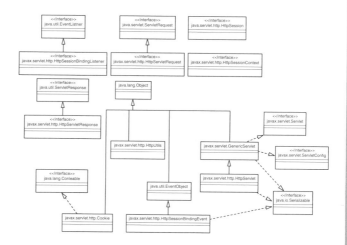

Figure 21.1

The javax.servlet.http *object model.*

Interfaces

Interfaces for the java.servlet.http package are HttpServletRequest, HttpServletResponse, HttpSession, and HttpSessionBindingListener.

HttpServletRequest Interface

```
public interface HttpServletRequest
  extends ServletRequest
```

The HttpServletRequest interface defines an object that provides the HttpServlet.service() method with access to HTTP-protocol–specific header information sent by the client. The HttpServletRequest interface has 26 methods, described in the following sections.

addHeader() Method

```
public void addHeader(java.lang.String name, java.lang.String value)
```

The addHeader() method adds another value to the response for the given header. addHeader() returns no value and throws no exceptions.

Parameters

- java.lang.String
- java.lang.String

addDateHeader() Method

```
public void addDateHeader(java.lang.String name, long date)
```

The addDateHeader() method adds another date value to the response for the given header. addDateHeader() returns no value and throws no exceptions.

Parameters

- java.lang.String
- long

addIntHeader() Method

```
public void addIntHeader(java.lang.String name, int value)
```

The addIntHeader() method adds another int value to the response for the given header. addIntHeader() returns no value and throws no exceptions.

Parameters

- java.lang.String
- int

getAuthType() Method

```
public java.lang.String getAuthType()
```

The getAuthType() method returns the authentication scheme used in this request. It is the same as the AUTH_TYPE CGI variable. getAuthType() has no parameters and throws no exceptions.

Returns

- java.lang.String

getContextPath() Method

public java.lang.String getContextPath()

The getContextPath() method returns the context path of this request. getContextPath() has no parameters and throws no exceptions.

Returns

- java.lang.String

getCookies() Method

public Cookie[] getCookies()

The getCookies() method returns an array of Cookie objects found in the client request. getCookies() has no parameters and throws no exceptions.

Returns

- Cookie[]

getDateHeader() Method

public long getDateHeader(java.lang.String name)

The getDateHeader() method returns the value of the requested date header field found in the client request. getDateHeader() throws no exceptions.

Parameters

- java.lang.String

Returns

- long

getHeader() Method

public java.lang.String getHeader(java.lang.String name)

The getHeader() method returns the value of the requested header field found in the client request. getHeader() throws no exceptions.

Parameters

- java.lang.String

Returns

- java.lang.String

getHeaders() Method

public Enumeration getHeaders(java.lang.String name)

The getHeaders() method returns an `Enumeration` of `Strings` containing all of the values for the given header. getHeaders() throws no exceptions.

Parameters

- java.lang.String

Returns

- Enumeration

getHeaderNames() Method

public Enumeration getHeaderNames()

The getHeaderNames() method returns an `Enumeration` containing all of the header names found in the client request. getHeaderNames() has no parameters and throws no exceptions.

Returns

- Enumeration

getIntHeader() Method

public int getIntHeader(java.lang.String name)

The getIntHeader() method returns the `int` value of the named header field, found in the client request. getIntHeader() throws no exceptions.

Parameters

- java.lang.String

Returns

- int

getMethod() Method

public java.lang.String getMethod()

The getMethod() method returns the HTTP method used by the client request. It is the same as the CGI variable `REQUEST_METHOD`. getMethod() has no parameters and throws no exceptions.

Returns

- java.lang.String

getPathInfo() Method

public java.lang.String getPathInfo()

The getPathInfo() method returns a `String` containing any additional path information following the servlet path, but preceding the query string. It is the same as the CGI variable `PATH_INFO`. getPathInfo() has no parameters and throws no exceptions.

Returns

- java.lang.String

getPathTranslated() Method

public java.lang.String getPathTranslated()

The getPathTranslated() method returns the same information as the getPathInfo() method, but translates the path to its real path name before returning it. It is the same as the CGI variable PATH_TRANSLATED. getPathTranslated() has no parameters and throws no exceptions.

Returns

- java.lang.String

getQueryString() Method

public java.lang.String getQueryString()

The getQueryString() method returns the query string from the request. It is the same as the CGI variable QUERY_STRING. getQueryString() has no parameters and throws no exceptions.

Returns

- java.lang.String

getRemoteUser() Method

public java.lang.String getRemoteUser()

The getRemoteUser() method returns the name of the user making the request. If the name is not available, null is returned. It is the same as the CGI variable REMOTE_USER. getRemoteUser() has no parameters and throws no exceptions.

Returns

- java.lang.String

getRequestedSessionId() Method

public java.lang.String getRequestedSessionId()

The getRequestedSessionId() method returns the session id associated with the request. getRequestedSessionId() has no parameters and throws no exceptions.

Returns

- java.lang.String

getRequestURI() Method

public java.lang.String getRequestURI()

The getRequestURI() method returns the first line of the request's URI. This is the part of the URI that is found to the left of the query string. getRequestURI() has no parameters and throws no exceptions.

Returns

- java.lang.String

getUserPrincipal() Method

`public java.security.Principal getUserPrincipal()`

The getUserPrincipal() method returns the Principal of the user making the request. getUserPrincipal() has no parameters and throws no exceptions.

Returns

- java.security.Principal

getServletPath() Method

`public java.lang.String getServletPath()`

The getServletPath() method returns the part of the URI that refers to the servlet being invoked. getServletPath() has no parameters and throws no exceptions.

Returns

- java.lang.String

getSession(boolean create) Method

`public HttpSession getSession(boolean create)`

The getSession() method returns the session associated with the request. If there is no valid session and the boolean parameter passed in is true, then it will create a new session. getSession() throws no exceptions.

Parameters

- boolean

Returns

- HttpSession

getSession() Method

`public HttpSession getSession()`

The getSession() method performs the same as the previous getSession() method; it just performs as if it was always passed a true value. getSession() has no parameters and throws no exceptions.

Returns

- HttpSession

isRequestedSessionValid() Method

```
public boolean isRequestedSessionValid()
```

The `isRequestedSessionValid()` method returns true if the session is valid in the current context; otherwise, it returns false. `isRequestedSessionValid()` has no parameters and throws no exceptions.

Returns

- `boolean`

isRequestedSessionFromCookie() Method

```
public boolean isRequestedSessionFromCookie()
```

The `isRequestedSessionFromCookie()` method returns true if the session id from the request came in as a cookie; otherwise, it returns false. `isRequestedSession FromCookie()` has no parameters and throws no exceptions.

Returns

- `boolean`

isRequestedSessionFromURL() Method

```
public boolean isRequestedSessionFromURL()
```

The `isRequestedSessionFromURL()` method returns true if the session id from the request came in as part of the URL; otherwise, it returns false. `isRequestedSession FromURL()` has no parameters and throws no exceptions.

Returns

- `boolean`

HttpServletResponse Interface

```
public interface HttpServletResponse
  extends ServletRequest
```

The `HttpServletResponse` interface defines an object that provides the `HttpServlet.service()` method with the capability to manipulate HTTP-protocol–specific header information and return data to the client. The `HttpServletResponse` interface has 39 fields and 10 methods, described in following sections.

SC_CONTINUE Field

```
public static final int SC_CONTINUE
```

This field represents a status code of (100), indicating that the client can continue.

SC_SWITCHING_PROTOCOLS Field

```
public static final int SC_SWITCHING_PROTOCOLS
```

This field represents a status code of (101), indicating the server is switching protocols according to the Upgrade header.

SC_OK Field

```
public static final int SC_OK
```

This field represents a status code of (200), indicating the request succeeded normally.

SC_CREATED Field

```
public static final int SC_CREATED
```

This field represents a status code of (201), indicating the request succeeded and created a new resource on the server.

SC_ACCEPTED Field

```
public static final int SC_ACCEPTED
```

This field represents a status code of (202), indicating that a request was accepted for processing, but was not completed.

SC_NON_AUTHORITATIVE_INFORMATION Field

```
public static final int SC_NON_AUTHORITATIVE_INFORMATION
```

This field represents a status code of (203), indicating that the meta information presented by the client did not originate from the server.

SC_NO_CONTENT Field

```
public static final int SC_NO_CONTENT
```

This field represents a status code of (204), indicating that the request succeeded but that there was no new information to return.

SC_RESET_CONTENT Field

```
public static final int SC_RESET_CONTENT
```

This field represents a status code of (205), indicating that the agent should reset the document view, which caused the request to be sent.

SC_PARTIAL_CONTENT Field

```
public static final int SC_PARTIAL_CONTENT
```

This field represents a status code of (206), indicating that the server has fulfilled the partial GET request for the resource.

SC_MULTIPLE_CHOICES Field

```
public static final int SC_MULTIPLE_CHOICES
```

This field represents a status code of (300), indicating that the requested resource corresponds to any one of a set of representations, each with its own specific location.

SC_MOVED_PERMANENTLY Field

`public static final int SC_MOVED_PERMANENTLY`

This field represents a status code of (301), indicating that the resource has permanently moved to a new location, and that future references should use a new URI with their requests.

SC_MOVED_TEMPORARILY Field

`public static final int SC_MOVED_TEMPORARILY`

This field represents a status code of (302), indicating that the resource has temporarily moved to another location, but that future references should still use the original URI to access the resource.

SC_SEE_OTHER Field

`public static final int SC_SEE_OTHER`

This field represents a status code of (303), indicating that the response to the request can be found under a different URI.

SC_NOT_MODIFIED Field

`public static final int SC_NOT_MODIFIED`

This field represents a status code of (304), indicating that a conditional GET operation found that the resource was available and not modified.

SC_USE_PROXY Field

`public static final int SC_USE_PROXY`

This field represents a status code of (305), indicating that the requested resource must be accessed through the proxy given by the Location field.

SC_BAD_REQUEST Field

`public static final int SC_BAD_REQUEST`

This field represents a status code of (400), indicating the request sent by the client was syntactically incorrect.

SC_UNAUTHORIZED Field

`public static final int SC_UNAUTHORIZED`

This field represents a status code of (401), indicating that the request requires HTTP authentication.

SC_PAYMENT_REQUIRED Field

```
public static final int SC_PAYMENT_REQUIRED
```

This field represents a status code of (402) for future use.

SC_FORBIDDEN Field

```
public static final int SC_FORBIDDEN
```

This field represents a status code of (403), indicating the server understood the request but refused to fulfill it.

SC_NOT_FOUND Field

```
public static final int SC_NOT_FOUND
```

This field represents a status code of (404), indicating that the requested resource is not available.

SC_METHOD_NOT_ALLOWED Field

```
public static final int SC_METHOD_NOT_ALLOWED
```

This field represents a status code of (405), indicating that the method specified in the Request-Line is not allowed for the resource identified by the Request-URI.

SC_NOT_ACCEPTABLE Field

```
public static final int SC_NOT_ACCEPTABLE
```

This field represents a status code of (406), indicating that the resource identified by the request is only capable of generating response entities which have content characteristics not acceptable according to the accept headers sent in the request.

SC_PROXY_AUTHENTICATION_REQUIRED Field

```
public static final int SC_PROXY_AUTHENTICATION_REQUIRED
```

This field represents a status code of (407), indicating that the client must first authenticate itself with the proxy.

SC_REQUEST_TIMEOUT Field

```
public static final int SC_REQUEST_TIMEOUT
```

This field represents a status code of (408), indicating that the client did not produce a request within the time that the server was prepared to wait.

SC_CONFLICT Field

```
public static final int SC_CONFLICT
```

This field represents a status code of (409), indicating that the request could not be completed due to a conflict with the current state of the resource.

SC_GONE Field

`public static final int SC_GONE`

This field represents a status code of (410), indicating that the resource is no longer available at the server and no forwarding address is known. This condition should be considered permanent.

SC_LENGTH_REQUIRED Field

`public static final int SC_LENGTH_REQUIRED`

This field represents a status code of (411), indicating that the request cannot be handled without a defined `Content-Length`.

SC_PRECONDITION_FAILED Field

`public static final int SC_PRECONDITION_FAILED`

This field represents a status code of (412), indicating that the precondition given in one or more of the request-header fields evaluated to false when it was tested on the server.

SC_REQUEST_ENTITY_TOO_LARGE Field

`public static final int SC_REQUEST_ENTITY_TOO_LARGE`

This field represents a status code of (413), indicating that the server is refusing to process the request because the request entity is larger than the server is willing or able to process.

SC_REQUEST_URI_TOO_LONG Field

`public static final int SC_REQUEST_URI_TOO_LONG`

This field represents a status code of (414), indicating that the server is refusing to service the request because the `Request-URI` is longer than the server is willing to interpret.

SC_UNSUPPORTED_MEDIA_TYPE Field

`public static final int SC_UNSUPPORTED_MEDIA_TYPE`

This field represents a status code of (415), indicating that the server is refusing to service the request because the entity of the request is in a format not supported by the requested resource for the requested method.

SC_INTERNAL_SERVER_ERROR Field

`public static final int SC_INTERNAL_SERVER_ERROR`

This field represents a status code of (500), indicating an error inside the HTTP server which prevented it from fulfilling the request.

SC_NOT_IMPLEMENTED Field

`public static final int SC_NOT_IMPLEMENTED`

This field represents a status code of (501), indicating the HTTP server does not support the functionality needed to fulfill the request.

SC_BAD_GATEWAY Field

`public static final int SC_BAD_GATEWAY`

This field represents a status code of (502), indicating that the HTTP server received an invalid response from a server it consulted when acting as a proxy or gateway.

SC_SERVICE_UNAVAILABLE Field

`public static final int SC_SERVICE_UNAVAILABLE`

This field represents a status code of (503), indicating that the HTTP server is temporarily overloaded, and unable to handle the request.

SC_GATEWAY_TIMEOUT Field

`public static final int SC_GATEWAY_TIMEOUT`

This field represents a status code of (504), indicating that the server did not receive a timely response from the upstream server while acting as a gateway or proxy.

SC_HTTP_VERSION_NOT_SUPPORTED Field

`public static final int SC_HTTP_VERSION_NOT_SUPPORTED`

This field represents a status code of (505), indicating that the server does not support or refuses to support the HTTP version found in the request.

addCookie() Method

`public void addCookie(Cookie cookie)`

The `addCookie()` method adds a `Cookie` to the `HttpServletResponse` object. `addCookie()` throws no exceptions. `addCookie()` returns no value.

Parameters

- `Cookie`

containsHeader() Method

`public boolean containsHeader(java.lang.String name)`

The `containsHeader()` method returns true if the named header exists in the response. `containsHeader()` throws no exceptions.

Parameters

- `java.lang.String`

Returns

- `boolean`

encodeURL() Method

`public java.lang.String encodeURL(java.lang.String url)`

The `encodeURL()` method's URL encodes the passed-in `String` and returns it. If no changes are necessary, then it simply returns the `String`. `encodeURL()` throws no exceptions.

Parameters

- `java.lang.String`

Returns

- `java.lang.String`

encodeRedirectURL() Method

`public java.lang.String encodeRedirectURL(java.lang.String url)`

The `encodeRedirectURL()` method's URL encodes the passed in `String` for use in the `sendRedirect()` method. If no changes are necessary, then it simply returns the `String`. `encodeRedirectURL()` throws no exceptions.

Parameters

- `java.lang.String`

Returns

- `java.lang.String`

sendError(int sc, java.lang.String message) Method

```
public void sendError(int sc,
  java.lang.String message)
throws java.io.IOException
```

The `sendError()` method sends an error to the client in the response object. The error consists of the `int` status code and a `String` message. `sendError()` returns no value.

Parameters

- `int`
- `java.lang.String`

Exceptions Thrown

- `java.io.IOException`

sendError(int sc) Method

```
public void sendError(int sc)
throws java.io.IOException
```

This `sendError()` method sends an error to the client in the response object. The error consists of only the `int` status code. `sendError()` returns no value.

Parameters

- `int`

Exceptions Thrown

- `java.io.IOException`

sendRedirect() Method

```
public void sendRedirect(java.lang.String url)
throws java.io.IOException
```

The `sendRedirect()` method redirects the client to the passed-in URL, which must be an absolute URL. `sendRedirect()` returns no value.

Parameters

- `java.lang.String`

Exceptions Thrown

- `java.io.IOException`

setDateHeader() Method

```
public void setDateHeader(java.lang.String name,
  long date)
```

The `setDateHeader()` method adds a name/date-value field to the response header. The date value is a `long` representing milliseconds since the epoch. `setDateHeader()` returns no value and throws no exception.

Parameters

- `java.lang.String`
- `long`

setIntHeader() Method

```
public void setIntHeader(java.lang.String name,
  int value)
```

The `setIntHeader()` method adds a name/int-value field to the response header. If the field is already present in the request, it is replaced. `setIntHeader()` returns no value and throws no exceptions.

Parameters

- `java.lang.String`
- `int`

setStatus() Method

```
public void setStatus(int sc)
```

The setStatus() method sets the status code for the response. setStatus() returns no value and throws no exceptions.

Parameters

- int

HttpSession Interface

```
public interface HttpSession
```

The HttpSession interface defines an object that provides an association between a client and server persisting over multiple connections. Using HttpSession gives you the ability to maintain state between transactions. This interface has 12 methods, described in the following sections.

getAttribute() Method

```
public java.lang.Object getAttribute(java.lang.String name)
```

The getAttribute() method returns a reference to the named object in the current session. The object must be downcasted to its original type. getAttribute() throws no exceptions.

Parameters

- java.lang.String

Returns

- java.lang.Object

getAttributeNames() Method

```
public Enumeration getAttributeNames()
```

The getAttributeNames() method returns an Enumeration of Strings representing all of the data objects bound to this session. getAttributeNames() has no parameters and throws no exceptions.

Returns

- Enumeration

getCreationTime() Method

```
public long getCreationTime()
```

The getCreationTime() method returns the time in which the session was created. This time value is a long representing the milliseconds elapsed since January 1, 1970 UTC. getCreationTime() has no parameters and throws no exceptions.

Returns

- long

getId() Method

```
public java.lang.String getId()
```

The getId() method returns a String containing a unique identifier for the current HttpSession. getId() has no parameters and throws no exceptions.

Returns

- java.lang.String

getLastAccessedTime() Method

```
public long getLastAccessedTime()
```

The getLastAccessedTime() method returns the last time, in milliseconds, the client sent a request with HttpSession. getLastAccessedTime() has no parameters and throws no exceptions.

Returns

- long

getMaxIntervalTime() Method

```
public int getMaxIntervalTime()
```

The getMaxIntervalTime() method returns the maximum interval between requests that the server will keep the session valid. getMaxIntervalTime() has no parameters and throws no exceptions.

Returns

- int

getSessionContext() Method

```
public HttpSessionContext getSessionContext()
```

The getSessionContext() method returns a reference to a HttpSessionContext object bound to the current session. getSessionContext() has no parameters and throws no exceptions.

Returns

- HttpSessionContext

invalidate() Method

```
public void invalidate()
```

The invalidate() method forces the session to be invalidated and removed from the context. invalidate() has no parameters, returns no value, and throws no exceptions.

isNew() Method

```
public boolean isNew()
```

The isNew() method returns true if the server has just created the session and the session has not been acknowledged by the client. isNew() has no parameters and throws no exceptions.

Returns

- boolean

setAttribute() Method

```
public void setAttribute(java.lang.String name)
  java.lang.Object value)
```

The setAttribute() method binds the passed-in object to the passed-in String and puts the object into the session. If there is an object in the session already bound to the name, it is replaced. setAttribute() returns no value and throws no exceptions.

Parameters

- java.lang.String
- java.lang.Object

removeAttribute() Method

```
public void removeAttribute(java.lang.String name)
```

The removeAttribute() method removes the object from the current session that is bound to the passed-in name. All objects implementing the HttpSessionBinding Listener interface will have their valueUnbound() methods called. removeAttribute() returns no value and throws no exceptions.

Parameters

- java.lang.String

setMaxIntervalTime() Method

```
public void setMaxIntervalTime(int interval)
```

The setMaxIntervalTime() method sets the maximum interval between requests before a server invalidates the session. setMaxIntervalTime() returns no value and throws no exceptions.

Parameters

- int

HttpSessionBindingListener Interface

```
public interface HttpSessionBindingListener
  extends java.util.EventListener
```

The HttpSessionBindingListener interface defines methods that an object can implement if it wants to be notified of an object in the session being bound or unbound. The HttpSessionBindingListener interface has two methods, described in the following sections.

valueBound() Method

```
public void valueBound(HttpSessionBindingEvent event)
```

The valueBound() method notifies a listener that the object is being bound into a session. valueBound() returns no value and throws no exceptions.

Parameters

- HttpSessionBindingEvent

valueUnBound() Method

```
public void valueUnBound(HttpSessionBindingEvent event)
```

The valueUnBound() method notifies a listener that the object is being unbound from a session. valueUnBound() returns no value and throws no exceptions.

Parameters

- HttpSessionBindingEvent

Classes

The four classes for the java.servlet.http package are Cookie, HttpServlet, HttpSessionBindingEvent, and HttpUtils.

Cookie Class

```
public class Cookie
  extends java.lang.Object
  implements java.lang.Cloneable
```

The Cookie class represents a cookie used for session management in HTTP protocols. Cookies are name/value pairs that are created by the server and stored in the client. The Cookie class has 17 methods, described in the following sections.

Cookie() Method

```
public Cookie(java.lang.String name,
  java.lang.String value)
```

The Cookie() constructor initializes a Cookie object with the passed-in name/value pair. Names cannot contain whitespace, commas, or semicolons and should only contain ASCII alphanumeric characters. Cookie() returns no value and throws no exceptions.

Parameters

- java.lang.String
- java.lang.String

setComment() Method

`public void setComment(java.lang.String purpose)`

The `setComment()` method is used to describe the cookie's purpose, when requested by the client. `setComment()` returns no value and throws no exceptions.

Parameters

- `java.lang.String`

getComment() Method

`public java.lang.String getComment()`

The `getComment()` method returns the comment used to describe the cookie's purpose. `getComment()` has no parameters and throws no exceptions.

Returns

- `java.lang.String`

setDomain() Method

`public void setDomain(java.lang.String pattern)`

The `setDomain()` method sets the pattern to match the host's domain. If the host does not match, then the cookie will not be presented to the host. `setDomain()` returns no value and throws no exceptions.

Parameters

- `java.lang.String`

getDomain() Method

`public java.lang.String getDomain()`

The `getDomain()` method returns the domain pattern of this cookie. `getDomain()` has no parameters and throws no exceptions.

Returns

- `java.lang.String`

setMaxAge() Method

`public void setMaxAge(int value)`

The `setMaxAge()` method sets the maximum age of the cookie. The cookie will expire after the passed-in number of seconds. `setMaxAge()` returns no value and throws no exceptions.

Parameters

- `int`

getMaxAge() Method

`public int getMaxAge()`

The `getMaxAge()` method returns the maximum age of the cookie in seconds. `getMaxAge()` has no parameters and throws no exceptions.

Returns

- `int`

setPath() Method

`public void setPath(java.lang.String uri)`

The `setPath()` method sets the valid path for the cookie. If the URL does not begin with the passed-in value, then it is not a valid path. `setPath()` returns no value and throws no exceptions.

Parameters

- `java.lang.String`

getPath() Method

`public java.lang.String getPath()`

The `getPath()` method returns the URL prefix for which this cookie is targeted. `getPath()` has no parameters and throws no exceptions.

Returns

- `java.lang.String`

setSecure() Method

`public void setSecure(boolean flag)`

The `setSecure()` method indicates to the user agent that the cookie should only be transmitted using a secure protocol. `setSecure()` returns no value and throws no exceptions.

Parameters

- `boolean`

getSecure() Method

`public boolean getSecure()`

The `getSecure()` method returns true if the cookie can only be transmitted using a secure protocol. `getSecure()` has no parameters and throws no exceptions.

Returns

- `boolean`

getName() Method

`public java.lang.String getName()`

The `getName()` method returns the name of the cookie. `getName()` has no parameters and throws no exceptions.

Returns

- `java.lang.String`

setValue() Method

`public void setValue(java.lang.String value)`

The `setValue()` method sets the value of the cookie. `setValue()` returns no value and throws no exceptions.

Parameters

- `java.lang.String`

getValue() Method

`public java.lang.String getValue()`

The `getValue()` method returns the value of the cookie. `getValue()` has no parameters and throws no exceptions.

Returns

- `java.lang.String`

getVersion() Method

`public int getVersion()`

The `getVersion()` method returns the version number of the cookie. A zero indicates that the cookie is based on the original specification developed by Netscape. A 1 indicates that the cookie is based on the RFC 2109. `getVersion()` has no parameters and throws no exceptions.

Returns

- `int`

setVersion() Method

`public void setVersion(int value)`

The `setVersion()` method sets the cookie protocol used when the cookie saves itself. `setVersion()` returns no value and throws no exceptions.

Parameters

- `int`

clone() Method

```
public java.lang.Object clone()
```

The clone() method returns a copy of this object. clone() has no parameters and throws no exceptions.

Returns

- java.lang.Object

HttpServlet Class

```
public class HttpServlet
  extends javax.servlet.GenericServlet
  implements java.io.Serializable
```

The HttpServlet class is meant to simplify the writing of HTTP servlets. It extends the GenericServlet class and implements the java.io.Serializable interface. The HttpServlet class is an abstract class; therefore, it cannot be instantiated directly. The HttpServlet class has 11 methods, described in the following sections.

HttpServlet() Method

```
public HttpServlet()
```

The HttpServlet() constructor is a default empty constructor. HttpServlet() has no parameters, returns no value, and throws no exceptions.

doGet() Method

```
protected void doGet(HttpServletRequest request,
  HttpServletResponse response)
  throws ServletException
  java.io.IOException
```

The doGet() method services all GET requests for the servlet.

NOTE

The HttpServlet class's doGet, doPost, doPut, doDelete, doOptions, and doTrace methods all receive the same two parameters—an HttpServletRequest object, which encapsulates the client's request, and an HttpServletResponse object, which contains the response that is sent back to the client. Each of these methods throws a ServletException if it cannot service the request and throws a java.io.IOException if there was an I/O error. These methods return no value.

doPost() Method

```
protected void doPost(HttpServletRequest request,
  HttpServletResponse response)
  throws ServletException
  java.io.IOException
```

The doPost() method services all POST requests for the servlet.

doPut() Method

```
protected void doPut(HttpServletRequest request,
  HttpServletResponse response)
  throws ServletException
  java.io.IOException
```

The doPut() method services all PUT requests for the servlet.

doDelete() Method

```
protected void doDelete(HttpServletRequest request,
  HttpServletResponse response)
  throws ServletException
  java.io.Exception
```

The doDelete() method services all DELETE requests for the servlet.

doOptions() Method

```
protected void doOptions(HttpServletRequest request,
  HttpServletResponse response)
  throws ServletException
  java.io.Exception
```

The doOptions() method services all OPTIONS requests for the servlet. The default implementation automatically determines what HTTP options are supported.

doTrace() Method

```
protected void doTrace(HttpServletRequest request,
  HttpServletResponse response)
  throws ServletException
  java.io.Exception
```

The doTrace() method services all TRACE requests for the servlet.

getLastModifiedTime() Method

```
protected long getLastModifiedTime(HttpServletRequest request)
```

The getLastModifiedTime() method returns the last time the requested entity was modified. The value returned is measured in milliseconds since January 1, 1970. getLastModifiedTime() throws no exceptions.

Parameters

- HttpServletRequest

Returns

- long

service(HttpServletRequest request, HttpServletResponse response) Method

```
protected void service(HttpServletRequest request,
  HttpServletResponse response)
  throws ServletException
  java.io.Exception
```

This is an HTTP-specific implementation of the `Servlet.service()` method. It handles standard HTTP requests by dispatching them to the appropriately implemented methods. The `service()` method throws a `ServletException` if it cannot service the request and throws a `java.io.IOException` if there was an I/O error. `service()` returns no value.

Parameters

- `HttpServletRequest`
- `HttpServletResponse`

Exceptions Thrown

- `ServletException`
- `java.io.IOException`

service(ServletRequest request, ServletResponse response) Method

```
public void service(ServletRequest request,
  ServletResponse response)
  throws ServletException
  java.io.Exception
```

This method implements the `Servlet.service()` method by delegating requests to the appropriate HTTP-specific `service()` method. The `service()` method throws a `ServletException` if it cannot service the request and throws a `java.io.IOException` if there was an I/O error. `service()` returns no value.

Parameters

- `ServletRequest`
- `ServletResponse`

Exceptions Thrown

- `ServletException`
- `java.io.IOException`

HttpSessionBindingEvent Class

```
public class HttpSessionBindingEvent
  extends java.util.EventObject
```

The HttpSessionBindingEvent class is sent, to all objects that implement the HttpSessionBindingListener, when a listener is bound or unbound from an HttpSession. The HttpSessionBindingEvent class has three methods, described in the following sections.

HttpSessionBindingEvent() Method

```
public HttpSessionBindingEvent(HttpSession session,
  java.lang.String name)
```

The HttpSessionBindingEvent() constructor initializes the object with the session acting as the source of the event and the name of the object being bound or unbound. HttpSessionBindingEvent() returns no value and throws no exceptions.

Parameters

- HttpSession
- java.lang.String

getName() Method

```
public java.lang.String getName()
```

The getName() method returns the name of the object that is being bound or unbound. getName() has no parameters and throws no exceptions.

Returns

- java.lang.String

getSession() Method

```
public HttpSession getSession()
```

The getSession() method returns the session from which the listener is being bound or unbound. getSession() has no parameters and throws no exceptions.

Returns

- HttpSession

HttpUtils Class

```
public class HttpUtils
  extends java.util.EventObject
```

The HttpUtils class contains a collection of static utility methods that are useful to HTTP servlets. The HttpUtils class has four methods, described in the following sections.

HttpUtils() Method

```
public HttpUtils()
```

The HttpUtils() constructor creates an empty HttpUtility object. HttpUtils() has no parameters, returns no value, and throws no exceptions.

parseQueryString() Method

```
public static java.util.Hashtable
  parseQueryString(java.lang.String s)
```

The parseQueryString() method takes the passed-in query string and parses it into a Hashtable of key/value pairs, where the values are arrays of strings. parseQueryString() throws no exceptions.

Parameters

- java.lang.String

Returns

- java.util.Hashtable

parsePostData() Method

```
public static java.util.Hashtable
  parsePostData(int len,
  ServletInputStream in)
```

The parsePostData() method takes HTML form data that is sent to the server as a POST request, parses it, and returns a Hashtable of key/value pairs. If keys have multiple values, their values are stored as an array of Strings. parsePostData() throws no exceptions.

Parameters

- int
- ServletInputStream

Returns

- java.util.Hashtable

getRequestURL() Method

```
public static java.lang.StringBuffer
  getRequestURL(HttpServletRequest request)
```

The getRequestURL() method takes a request object and reconstructs the URL used by the client to make the request. getRequestURL() throws no exceptions.

Parameters

- HttpServletRequest

Returns

- java.lang.StringBuffer

INDEX

A

C

characters() method, 170
classes
GenericServlet class, 23-24
HttpServlet class, 23-24
InternetAddress class, 189
javax.servlet package, 258-265
GenericServlet, 258-261
ServletInputStream, 261
ServletOutputStream,
261-265
javax.servlet.http package,
286-294
Cookie class, 286-290
HttpServlet class, 290-292
HttpSessionBindingEvent
class, 293
HttpUtils class, 293-294
javax.servlet.jsp package, 199-217
JspEngineInfo, 199
JspFactory, 199-201
JspWriter, 201-208
PageContext, 208-217
javax.servlet.jsp.tagext package,
219-239
BodyJspWriter class, 220
Tag class, 221-226
TagAttributeInfo class,
227-228
TagData class, 228-229
TagExtraInfo class, 230-231
TagInfo class, 231-234
TagLibraryInfo class, 235-
237
VariableInfo class, 237-239
Message abstract class, 189
MimeMessage class, 189
Model-View-Controller design
pattern (MVC), 175
Session class, 188-189

**className field (VariableInfo class),
237**
clear() method (JspWriter class), 207
**clearBody() method (BodyJspWriter
class), 220**
**clearbuffer() method (JspWriter
class), 207**
clone() method (Cookie class), 290
close() method (JspWriter class), 207
**code attribute (<jsp:plugin> action),
119**
code listings
AddToShoppingCart.jsp, 144
AddToShoppingCartMVC.jsp, 177
Applet1.java, 119
ApplicationBean1.jsp, 129
ApplicationBean2.jsp, 130
BasicServlet.html, 28
BasicServlet.java, 26
BeanCounter.jsp, 39
Company.java, 137
ConnectionPool.java, 153
Counter.java, 38, 123
CreateForm.jsp, 135
CreateTablesApp.java, 52
EmployeeInfo.jsp, 111
errorpage.jsp, 78
GetFromApplication.jsp, 104
header.jsp, 110
InsertDataApp.java, 54, 56
item.xml, 165
JDBCExample.jsp, 62-64
MailExample.jsp, 191
MailForm.html, 190
MCPHome.jsp, 116
PageBean.jsp, 124
PooledConnection.java, 151
PureJSPBase.java, 92
RequestBean1.jsp, 125
RetrieveFormData.jsp, 139
SamsHome.jsp, 116

H

U

V-W

X-Y-Z